# Laws of
# Duplicate
# Contract Bridge

*American Edition*

As Promulgated in the Western Hemisphere
by the
**AMERICAN CONTRACT BRIDGE LEAGUE**

Effective May 27, 1997

Published and distributed by the
American Contract Bridge League.

Library of Congress Catalog Card Number: 87-700085
ISBN: 0-943855-16-0
Dewey Classification 795.41

Published and distributed by the
American Contract Bridge League

# PREFACE TO THE
# NORTH AMERICAN EDITION
# LAWS OF DUPLICATE
# CONTRACT BRIDGE 1997

The first Laws of Duplicate Contract Bridge were published in 1928. There have been successive revisions in 1933, 1935, 1943, 1949, 1963, 1975 and 1987.

Through the Thirties, the Laws were promulgated by the Portland Club of London and the Whist Club of New York. From the Forties onwards, the American Contract Bridge League Laws Commission has replaced the Whist Club, while the British Bridge League and the European Bridge League supplemented the Portland Club's efforts. The 1975 Laws were also promulgated by the World Bridge Federation Laws Commission, as they have been in 1987 and the current version.

This latest revision supersedes the 1987 Code on September 1, 1997. Zonal authorities may implement the new Code any time after March 1, 1997. In the American Contract Bridge League the revised laws are effective on May 27, 1997.

In the 1975 Laws and prior, words such as may, should, shall and must were used without much discrimination; in 1987 they were rationalized, and the practice is continued in the current Laws. When these Laws say that a player "may" do something ("any player may call attention to an irregularity during the auction"), the failure to do it is in no way wrong. A simple declaration that a player "does" something (". . . dummy spreads his hand in front of him . . . ") establishes correct procedure without any suggestion that a violation be penalized. When a player "should" do something ("a claim should be accompanied at once by a statement . . ."), his failure to do it is an infraction of law, which will jeopardize his rights, but which will incur a procedural penalty only seldom. In contrast, when these Laws say that a player "shall" do something ("No player shall take any action until the Director has explained . . ."), a violation will be penalized more often than not. The strongest word, "must" ("before making a call, he must inspect the face of his cards"), indicates that violation is regarded as serious indeed. Note that "may" becomes very strong in the negative: "may not" is a stronger injunction than "shall not", just short of "must not."

A great deal of effort has been expended to make these Laws easy to use. References from one law to another have been made more explicit. The hundreds of headings and sub-headings can help a Director find the section of a law that is applicable to the facts of a case (these headings are for convenience of reference only; headings are not considered to be part of the Laws). The Table of Contents at the front of the book and the alphabetical index at the back should make a Director's task lighter.

The Drafting Committee notes with sorrow the passing of many previous contributors to the Laws whose imprint remains in the new Code — Jean Besse and Colin Harding of the WBF Laws Committee, and B. Jay Becker, Easley Blackwood and Alfred Sheinwold of the ACBL Laws Commission. We also acknowledge the efforts of Stewart Wheeler of the Portland Club for his help and advice.

The Drafting Committee acknowledges with gratitude the work of Rena Hetzer, who acted as secretary and liaison in the preparation of this revision.

# Promulgating Bodies

## THE LAWS COMMISSION
of the American Contract Bridge League
**EDGAR KAPLAN**, Co-Chairman
**RALPH COHEN**, Co-Chairman

## DRAFTING COMMITTEE
**EDGAR KAPLAN**, Chairman

## THE LAWS COMMISSION OF
## THE WORLD BRIDGE FEDERATION
**EDGAR KAPLAN**, Chairman (USA)

Ralph Cohen, Vice Chairman (USA)
Ton Kooijman, Vice Chairman (NETHERLANDS)

# Contents

## CHAPTER V — THE AUCTION
### PART ONE — CORRECT PROCEDURE
### SECTION ONE — AUCTION PERIOD

## SECTION THREE – INSUFFICIENT BID

## SECTION FOUR – CALL OUT OF ROTATION

## SECTION FIVE – INADMISSIBLE CALLS

## SECTION SIX – CONVENTIONS AND AGREEMENTS

## CHAPTER VI – THE PLAY
### PART ONE – PROCEDURE
### SECTION ONE – CORRECT PROCEDURE

## SECTION TWO – IRREGULARITIES IN PROCEDURE

## PART TWO – PENALTY CARD

## PART THREE – IRREGULAR LEADS AND PLAYS
## SECTION ONE – LEAD OUT OF TURN

## CHAPTER VII — PROPRIETIES

## CHAPTER VIII — THE SCORE

# CHAPTER IX — TOURNAMENT SPONSORSHIP

# CHAPTER X — TOURNAMENT DIRECTOR
## SECTION ONE — RESPONSIBILITIES

## SECTION TWO — RULINGS

## SECTION THREE — CORRECTION OF IRREGULARITIES

# The Scope of the Laws

The Laws are designed to define correct procedure, and to provide an adequate remedy when there is a departure from correct procedure. An offending player should be ready to pay any penalty graciously, or to accept any adjusted score awarded by the Tournament Director. The Laws are primarily designed not as punishment for irregularities, but rather as redress for damage.

# CHAPTER I

# Definitions

*Adjusted Score* — An arbitrary score awarded by the Director (see Law 12). It is either "artificial" or "assigned". 1.
An artificial adjusted score is one awarded in lieu of a
result because no result can be obtained or estimated for
a particular deal (*e.g.*, when an irregularity prevents play
of a deal). 2. An assigned adjusted score is awarded to
one side, or to both sides, to be the result of the deal in
place of the result actually obtained after an irregularity.

*Alert* — A notification, whose form may be specified by a
sponsoring organization, to the effect that opponents may
be in need of an explanation.

*Auction* — 1. The process of determining the contract by
means of successive calls. 2. The aggregate of calls made
(see Law 17E).

*Bid* — An undertaking to win at least a specified number of
odd tricks in a specified denomination.

*Board* — 1. A duplicate board as described in Law 2. 2.
The four hands as originally dealt and placed in a duplicate board for play during that session.

*Call* — Any bid, double, redouble or pass.

*Contestant* — In an individual event, a player; in a pair event,
two players playing as partners throughout the event; in
a team event, four or more players playing as teammates.

*Contract* — The undertaking by declarer's side to win, at
the denomination named, the number of odd tricks specified in the final bid, whether undoubled, doubled or redoubled.

*Convention* — 1. A call that, by partnership agreement,
conveys a meaning other than willingness to play in the
denomination named (or in the last denomination named),
or high-card strength or length (three cards or more)
there. However, an agreement as to overall strength does
not make a call a convention. 2. Defender's play that
serves to convey a meaning by agreement rather than
inference.

*Deal* — 1. The distribution of the pack to form the hands of the four players. 2. The cards so distributed considered as a unit, including the auction and play thereof.

*Declarer* — The player who, for the side that makes the final bid, first bid the denomination named in the final bid. He becomes declarer when the opening lead is faced (but see Law 54A when the opening lead is made out of turn).

*Defender* — An opponent of (presumed) declarer.

*Denomination* — The suit or notrump specified in a bid.

*Director* — A person designated to supervise a duplicate bridge contest and to apply these Laws.

*Double* — A call over an opponent's bid increasing the scoring value of fulfilled or defeated contracts (see Laws 19 and 77).

*Dummy* — 1. Declarer's partner. He becomes dummy when the opening lead is faced. 2. Declarer's partner's cards, once they are spread on the table after the opening lead.

*Event* — A contest of one or more sessions.

*Follow Suit* — Play a card of the suit that has been led.

*Game* — 100 or more trick points scored on one deal.

*Hand* — The cards originally dealt to a player, or the remaining portion thereof.

*Honor* — Any Ace, King, Queen, Jack or 10.

*International Matchpoint (IMP)* — A unit of scoring awarded according to a schedule established in Law 78B.

*Irregularity* — A deviation from the correct procedures set forth in the Laws.

*Lead* — The first card played to a trick.

*LHO* — Left-hand opponent.

*Matchpoint* — A unit of scoring awarded to a contestant as a result of comparison with one or more other scores.

*Odd Trick* — Each trick to be won by declarer's side in excess of six.

*Opening Lead* — The card led to the first trick.

*Opponent* — A player of the other side; a member of the partnership to which one is opposed.

*Overtrick* — Each trick won by declarer's side in excess of the contract.

*Pack* — The 52 playing cards with which the game of Contract Bridge is played.

*Partner* — The player with whom one plays as a side against the other two players.

*Partscore* — 90 or fewer trick points scored on one deal.

*Pass* — A call specifying that a player does not, at that turn, elect to bid, double or redouble.

*Play* — 1. The contribution of a card from one's hand to a trick, including the first card, which is the lead. 2. The aggregate of plays made. 3. The period during which the cards are played. 4. The aggregate of the calls and plays on a board.

*Premium Points* — Any points earned other than trick points (see Law 77).

*Psychic Call* — A deliberate and gross misstatement of honor strength or suit length.

*Rectification* — Adjustment made to permit the auction or play to proceed as normally as possible after an irregularity has occurred.

*Redouble* — A call over an opponent's double, increasing the scoring value of fulfilled or defeated contracts (see Laws 19 and 77).

*Revoke* — The play of a card of another suit by a player who is able to follow suit or to comply with a lead penalty.

*RHO* — Right-hand opponent.

*Rotation* — The clockwise order in which the deal and the right to call or play progress.

*Round* — A part of a session played without progression of players.

*Session* — An extended period of play during which a number of boards, specified by the sponsoring organization, is scheduled to be played.

*Side* — Two players who constitute a partnership against the other two players.

*Slam* — A contract to win six odd tricks (called Small Slam), or to win seven odd tricks (called Grand Slam).

*Suit* — One of four groups of cards in the pack, each group comprising thirteen cards and having a characteristic symbol: spades (♠), hearts (♥), diamonds (♦), clubs (♣).

*Team* — Two or more pairs playing in different directions at different tables, but for a common score (applicable regulations may permit teams of more than four members).

*Trick* — The unit by which the outcome of the contract is determined, regularly consisting of four cards, one contributed by each player in rotation, beginning with the lead.

*Trick Points* — Points scored by declarer's side for fulfilling the contract (see Law 77).

*Trump* — Each card of the suit, if any, named in the contract.

*Turn* — The correct time at which a player may call or play.

*Undertrick* — Each trick by which declarer's side falls short of fulfilling the contract (see Law 77).

*Vulnerability* — The conditions for assigning premiums and undertrick penalties (see Law 77).

# CHAPTER II

# Preliminaries

## LAW 1

### THE PACK — RANK OF CARDS AND SUITS

Duplicate Contract Bridge is played with a pack of 52 cards, consisting of 13 cards in each of four suits. The suits rank downward in the order spades (♠), hearts (♥), diamonds (♦), clubs (♣). The Cards of each suit rank downward in the order Ace, King, Queen, Jack, 10, 9, 8, 7, 6, 5, 4, 3, 2.

## LAW 2

### THE DUPLICATE BOARDS

A duplicate board containing a pack is provided for each deal to be played during a session. Each board is numbered and has four pockets to hold the four hands, designated North, East, South and West. The dealer and vulnerability are designated as follows:

| | | | | | |
|---|---|---|---|---|---|
| North Dealer | Boards | 1 | 5 | 9 | 13 |
| East Dealer | Boards | 2 | 6 | 10 | 14 |
| South Dealer | Boards | 3 | 7 | 11 | 15 |
| West Dealer | Boards | 4 | 8 | 12 | 16 |
| | | | | | |
| Neither Side Vulnerable | Boards | 1 | 8 | 11 | 14 |
| North–South Vulnerable | Boards | 2 | 5 | 12 | 15 |
| East–West Vulnerable | Boards | 3 | 6 | 9 | 16 |
| Both Sides Vulnerable | Boards | 4 | 7 | 10 | 13 |

The same sequence is repeated for Boards 17–32 and for each subsequent group of 16 boards.

No board that fails to conform to these conditions should be used. If such board is used, however, the conditions marked on it apply for that session.

## LAW 3

## ARRANGEMENT OF TABLES

Four players play at each table, and tables are numbered in a sequence established by the Director. He designates one direction as North; other compass directions assume the normal relationship to North.

## LAW 4

## PARTNERSHIPS

The four players at each table constitute two partnerships or sides, North–South against East–West. In pair or team events the contestants enter as pairs or teams and retain the same partnerships throughout a session (except in the case of substitutions authorized by the Director). In individual events each player enters separately, and partnerships change during a session.

# LAW 5

# ASSIGNMENT OF SEATS

A. Initial Position

The Director assigns an initial position to each contestant (individual, pair or team) at the start of a session. Unless otherwise directed, the members of each pair or team may select seats among those assigned to them by mutual agreement. Having once selected a compass direction, a player may change it within a session only upon instruction or with permission of the Director.

B. Change of Direction or Table

Players change their initial compass direction or proceed to another table in accordance with the Director's instructions. The Director is responsible for clear announcement of instructions; each player is responsible for moving when and as directed and for occupying the correct seat after each change.

# CHAPTER III

# Preparation and Progression

## LAW 6

## THE SHUFFLE AND DEAL

A. The Shuffle
   Before play starts, each pack is thoroughly shuffled. There is a cut if either opponent so requests.

B. The Deal
   The cards must be dealt face down, one card at time, into four hands of thirteen cards each; each hand is then placed face down in one of the four pockets of the board. The recommended procedure is that the cards be dealt in rotation, clockwise.

C. Representation of Both Pairs
   A member of each side should be present during the shuffle and deal unless the Director instructs otherwise.

D. New Shuffle and Redeal
   1. Cards Incorrectly Dealt or Exposed
      There must be a new shuffle and a redeal if it is ascertained before the auction begins for both sides (see Law 17A) that the cards have been incorrectly dealt or that a player could have seen the face of a card belonging to another hand.
   2. No Shuffle or No Deal
      No result may stand if the cards are dealt without shuffle from a sorted deck or if the deal had previously been played in a different session.
   3. At Director's Instruction
      Subject to Law 22A, there must be a new shuffle and

a redeal when required by the Director for any reason compatible with the Laws (but see Law 86C).

E. Director's Option on Shuffling and Dealing

1. By Players

   The Director may instruct that the shuffle and deal be performed at each table immediately before play starts.

2. By Director

   The Director may perform the shuffle and deal in advance, himself.

3. By Agents or Assistants

   The Director may have his assistants or other appointed agents perform the shuffle and deal in advance.

4. Different Method of Dealing or Pre-dealing

   The Director may require a different method of dealing or pre-dealing.

F. Duplication of Board

   If required by the conditions of play, one or more exact copies of each original deal may be made under the Director's instructions.

# LAW 7

# CONTROL OF BOARD AND CARDS

A. Placement of Board

   When a board is to be played it is placed in the center of the table until play is completed.

B. Removal of Cards from Board

   Each player takes a hand from the pocket corresponding to his compass position.

1. Counting Cards in Hand before Play
   Each player counts his cards face down to be sure he
   has exactly thirteen; after that, and before making a
   call, he must inspect the face of his cards.
2. Control of Player's Hand
   During play each player retains possession of his own
   cards, not permitting them to be mixed with those of
   any other player. No player shall touch any cards other
   than his own (but declarer may play dummy's cards in
   accordance with Law 45) during or after play except
   by permission of the Director.

C. Returning Cards to Board
   Each player shall restore his original thirteen cards to
   the pocket corresponding to his compass position. Thereafter no hand shall be removed from the board unless a
   member of each side, or the Director, is present.

D. Responsibility for Procedures
   Any contestant remaining at a table throughout a session is primarily responsible for maintaining proper conditions of play at the table.

# LAW 8

# SEQUENCE OF ROUNDS

A. Movement of Boards and Players
   1. Director's Instructions
      The Director instructs the players as to the proper
      movement of boards and progression of contestants.
   2. Responsibility for Moving Boards
      The North player at each table is responsible for mov-
      ing the boards just completed at his table to the proper
      table for the following round, unless the Director in-

structs otherwise.

B. End of Round

In general, a round ends when the Director gives the signal for the start of the following round; but if any table has not completed play by that time, the round continues for that table until there has been a progression of players.

C. End of Last Round and End of Session

The last round of a session, and the session itself, ends for each table when play of all boards scheduled at that table has been completed, and when all scores have been entered on the proper scoring forms without objection.

CHAPTER IV

# **General Laws Governing Irregularities**

## LAW 9

### PROCEDURE FOLLOWING AN IRREGULARITY

A. Calling Attention to an Irregularity
   1. During the Auction Period
      Unless prohibited by Law, any player may call attention to an irregularity during the auction, whether or not it is his turn to call.
   2. During the Play Period
      (a) Unless prohibited by Law, declarer or either defender may call attention to an irregularity that occurs during the play period.
      (b) Dummy (dummy's restricted rights are defined in Laws 42 and 43)
         (1) Dummy may not call attention to an irregularity during the play but may do so after play of the hand is concluded.
         (2) Dummy may attempt to prevent declarer from committing an irregularity (Law 42B2).

B. After Attention Is Called to an Irregularity
   1. Summoning the Director
      (a) When to Summon
         The Director must be summoned at once when attention is drawn to an irregularity.
      (b) Who May Summon
         Any player, including dummy, may summon the Director after attention has been drawn to an irregularity.
      (c) Retention of Rights

Summoning the Director does not cause a player to forfeit any rights to which he might otherwise be entitled.

(d) Opponents' Rights
The fact that a player draws attention to an irregularity committed by his side does not affect the rights of the opponents.

2. Further Bids or Plays
No player shall take any action until the Director has explained all matters in regard to rectification and to the assessment of a penalty.

C. Premature Correction of an Irregularity
Any premature correction of an irregularity by the offender may subject him to a further penalty (see the lead penalties of Law 26).

# LAW 10

# ASSESSMENT OF A PENALTY

A. Right to Assess Penalty
The Director alone has the right to assess penalties when applicable. Players do not have the right to assess (or waive) penalties on their own initiative.

B Cancellation of Payment or Waiver of Penalty
The Director may allow or cancel any payment or waiver of penalties made by the players without his instructions.

C. Choice after Irregularity
1. Explanation of Options
When these Laws provide an option after an irregularity, the Director shall explain all the options available.
2. Choice among Options

If a player has an option after an irregularity, he must make his selection without consulting partner.

# LAW 11

## FORFEITURE OF THE RIGHT TO PENALIZE

A. Action by Non-Offending Side

The right to penalize an irregularity may be forfeited if either member of the non-offending side takes any action before summoning the Director. The Director so rules when the non-offending side may have gained through subsequent action taken by an opponent in ignorance of the penalty.

B. Irregularity Called by Spectator
   1. Spectator Responsibility of Non-Offending Side
      The right to penalize an irregularity may be forfeited if attention is first drawn to the irregularity by a spectator for whose presence at the table the non-offending side is responsible.
   2. Spectator Responsibility of Offending Side
      The right to correct an irregularity may be forfeited if attention is first drawn to the irregularity by a spectator for whose presence at the table the offending side is responsible.

C. Penalty after Forfeiture of the Right to Penalize
   Even after the right to penalize has been forfeited under this Law, the Director may assess a procedural penalty (see Law 90).

# LAW 12

## DIRECTOR'S DISCRETIONARY POWERS

A. Right to Award an Adjusted Score

The Director may award an adjusted score (or scores), either on his own initiative or on the application of any player, but only when these Laws empower him to do so, or:

1. Laws Provide No Indemnity

   The Director may award an assigned adjusted score when he judges that these Laws do not provide indemnity to the non-offending contestant for the particular type of violation of law committed by an opponent.

2. Normal Play of the Board Is Impossible

   The Director may award an artificial adjusted score if no rectification can be made that will permit normal play of the board (see Law 88).

3. Incorrect Penalty Has Been Paid

   The Director may award an adjusted score if an incorrect penalty has been paid.

B. No Adjustment for Undue Severity of Penalty

The Director may not award an adjusted score on the ground that the penalty provided in these Laws is either unduly severe or advantageous to either side.

C. Awarding an Adjusted Score

1. Artificial Score

   When, owing to an irregularity, no result can be obtained, the Director awards an artificial adjusted score according to responsibility for the irregularity: average minus ( at most 40% of the available matchpoints in pairs) to a contestant directly at fault; average (50% in pairs) to a contestant only partially at fault; average plus (at least 60% in pairs ) to a contestant in no way at fault (see Law 86 for team play or Law 88 for pairs play). The scores awarded to the two sides need not balance.

2. Assigned Score

When the Director awards an assigned adjusted score in place of a result actually obtained after an irregularity, the score is, for a non-offending side, the most favorable result that was likely had the irregularity not occurred or, for an offending side, the most unfavorable result that was at all probable. The scores awarded to the two sides need not balance and may be assigned either in matchpoints or by altering the total-point score prior to matchpointing.

3. Unless Zonal Organizations specify otherwise, an appeals committee may vary an assigned adjusted score in order to do equity.

# LAW 13

## INCORRECT NUMBER OF CARDS

When the Director determines that one or more pockets of the board contained an incorrect number of cards,* and a player with an incorrect hand has made a call, then when the Director deems that the deal can be corrected and played normally with no change of call, the deal may be so played with the concurrence of all four players. Otherwise, the Director shall award an artificial adjusted score and may penalize an offender. If no such call has been made, then:

---

*Where three hands are correct and one hand is deficient, Law 14, and not this Law, applies.

A. No Player Has Seen Another's Card
   The Director shall correct the discrepancy as follows and, if no player will then have seen another's card, shall require that the board be played normally.
   1. Hand Records
      When hand records are available, the Director shall distribute the cards in accordance with the records.
   2. Consult Previous Players
      If hand records are not available, the Director shall correct the board by consulting with players who have previously played it.
   3. Require a Redeal
      If the board was incorrectly dealt, the Director shall require a redeal (Law 6).

B. A Player Has Seen Another Player's Card(s)
   When the Director determines that one or more pockets of the board contained an incorrect number of cards and after restoration of the board to its original condition a player has seen one or more cards of another player's hand, if the Director deems:
   1. The Information Gained Is Inconsequential
      that such information will not interfere with normal bidding or play, the Director, with the concurrence of all four players, may allow the board to be played and scored normally.
   2. The Information Will Interfere with Normal Play
      that the information gained thereby is of sufficient importance to interfere with normal bidding or play, or if any player objects to playing the board, the Director shall award an artificial adjusted score and may penalize an offender.

C. Play Completed
   When it is determined after play ends that a player's hand originally contained more than 13 cards with another player holding correspondingly fewer, the result must be

cancelled (for procedural penalty, see Law 90).

# LAW 14

## MISSING CARD

A. Hand Found Deficient before Play Commences
   When three hands are correct and the fourth is found to be deficient before the play period begins, the Director makes a search for any missing card, and:
   1. Card Is Found
      If a card is found, it is restored to the deficient hand.
   2. Card Cannot Be Found
      If a card cannot be found, the Director reconstructs the deal, as near to its original form as he can determine, by substituting another pack.

B. Hand Found Deficient Afterwards
   When three hands are correct and the fourth is found to be deficient after the play period begins, the Director makes a search for any missing card, and:
   1. Card Is Found
      (a) If a card is found among the played cards, Law 67 applies.
      (b) If a card is found elsewhere, it is restored to the deficient hand, and penalties may apply (see 3., following).
   2. Card Cannot Be Found
      If a card cannot be found, the deal is reconstructed as nearly as can be determined in its original form by substituting another pack, and penalties may apply (see 3., following).
   3. Possible Penalties
      A card restored to a hand under the provisions of Section B of this Law is deemed to have belonged con-

tinuously to the deficient hand. It may become a penalty card (Law 50), and failure to have played it may constitute a revoke.

## LAW 15

## PLAY OF A WRONG BOARD

A. Players Have Not Previously Played Board
   If players play a board not designated for them to play in the current round:
   1. Score Board as Played
      The Director normally allows the score to stand if none of the four players have previously played the board.
   2. Designate a Late Play
      The Director may require both pairs to play the correct board against one another later.

B. One or More Players Have Previously Played Board
   If any player plays a board he has previously played, with the correct opponents or otherwise, his second score on the board is cancelled both for his side and his opponents, and the Director shall award an artificial adjusted score to the contestants deprived of the opportunity to earn a valid score.

C. Discovered during Auction
   If, during the auction period, the Director discovers that a contestant is playing a board not designated for him to play in the current round, he shall cancel the auction, ensure that the correct contestants are seated and that they are informed of their rights both now and at future rounds. A second auction begins. Players must repeat calls they made previously. If any call differs in any way from the corresponding call in the first auction, the Di-

rector shall cancel the board. Otherwise, play continues normally.

# LAW 16

## UNAUTHORIZED INFORMATION

Players are authorized to base their calls and plays on information from legal calls and or plays, and from mannerisms of opponents. To base a call or play on other extraneous information may be an infraction of law.

A. Extraneous Information from Partner
   After a player makes available to his partner extraneous information that may suggest a call or play, as by means of a remark, a question, a reply to a question, or by unmistakable hesitation, unwonted speed, special emphasis, tone, gesture, movement, mannerism or the like, the partner may not choose from among logical alternative actions one that could demonstrably have been suggested over another by the extraneous information.
   1. When Such Information Is Given
      When a player considers that an opponent has made such information available and that damage could well result, he may, unless the regulations of the sponsoring organization prohibit, immediately announce that he reserves the right to summon the Director later (the opponents should summon the Director immediately if they dispute the fact that unauthorized information might have been conveyed).
   2. When Illegal Alternative Is Chosen
      When a player has substantial reason to believe* that an opponent who had a logical alternative has chosen an

---

*When play ends; or, as to dummy's hand, when dummy is exposed.

action that could have been suggested by such information, he should summon the Director forthwith. The Director shall require the auction and play to continue, standing ready to assign an adjusted score if he considers that an infraction of law has resulted in damage.

B. Extraneous Information from Other Sources

When a player accidentally receives unauthorized information about a board he is playing or has yet to play, as by looking at the wrong hand; by overhearing calls, results or remarks; by seeing cards at another table; or by seeing a card belonging to another player at his own table before the auction begins, the Director should be notified forthwith, preferably by the recipient of the information. If the Director considers that the information could interfere with normal play, he may:

1. Adjust Positions

   if the type of contest and scoring permit, adjust the players' positions at the table, so that the player with information about one hand will hold that hand; or,

2. Appoint Substitute

   with the concurrence of all four players, appoint a temporary substitute to replace the player who received the unauthorized information; or,

3. Award an Adjusted Score

   forthwith award an artificial adjusted score.

C. Information from Withdrawn Calls and Plays

A call or play may be withdrawn, and another substituted, either by a non-offending side after an opponent's infraction or by an offending side to rectify an infraction.

1. Non-offending Side

   For the non-offending side, all information arising from a withdrawn action is authorized, whether the action be its own or its opponents'.

2. Offending Side

   For the offending side, information arising from its
   own withdrawn action and from withdrawn actions of
   the non-offending side is unauthorized. A player of
   the offending side may not choose from among logical alternative actions one that could demonstrably
   have been suggested over another by the unauthorized information.

# CHAPTER V

# The Auction

## PART I
## CORRECT PROCEDURE

### SECTION ONE
### AUCTION PERIOD

#### LAW 17

#### DURATION OF THE AUCTION

A. Auction Period Starts

The auction period on a deal begins for a side when either partner looks at the face of his cards.

B. The First Call

The player designated by the board as dealer makes the first call.

C. Successive Calls

The player to dealer's left makes the second call, and thereafter each player calls in turn in a clockwise rotation.

D. Cards from Wrong Board

If a player who has inadvertently picked up the cards from a wrong board makes a call, that call is canceled. If offender's LHO has called over the canceled call, the Director shall assign artificial adjusted scores (see Law 90 for penalty) when offender's substituted call differs in any significant way from his canceled call. If offender subsequently repeats the canceled call on the board from which he mistakenly drew his cards, the Director may allow that board to be played normally*, but the Director shall assign artificial adjusted scores (see Law 90) when offender's call differs in any way from his original canceled call.

E. End of Auction Period
The auction period ends when all four players pass or when after three passes in rotation have followed any call the opening lead is faced (when a pass out of rotation has been accepted, see Law 34).

# LAW 18

## BIDS

A. Proper Form
A bid names a number of odd tricks, from one to seven, and a denomination. (Pass, double and redouble are calls but not bids.)

B. To Supersede a Bid
A bid supersedes a previous bid if it names either the same number of odd tricks in a higher-ranking denomination or a greater number of odd tricks in any denomination.

C. Sufficient Bid
A bid that supersedes the immediately previous bid is a sufficient bid.

D. Insufficient Bid
A bid that fails to supersede the immediately previous bid is an insufficient bid.

E. Rank of the Denominations
The rank of the denominations in descending order is:

---

*Offender's LHO must repeat the previous call.

notrump, spades, hearts, diamonds, clubs.

F. Different Methods

Zonal Organizations may authorize different methods of making calls.

## LAW 19

## DOUBLES AND REDOUBLES

A. Doubles
   1. Legal Double

      A player may double only the last preceding bid. That bid must have been made by an opponent; calls other than pass must not have intervened.
   2. Proper Form for Double

      In doubling, a player should not state the number of odd tricks or the denomination. The only correct form is the single word "Double".
   3. Double of Incorrectly Stated Bid

      If a player, in doubling, incorrectly states the bid, or the number of odd tricks or the denomination, he is deemed to have doubled the bid as it was made. (Law 16 – Unauthorized Information – may apply.)

B. Redoubles
   1. Legal Redouble

      A player may redouble only the last preceding double. That double must have been made by an opponent; calls other than pass must not have intervened.
   2. Proper Form for a Redouble

      In redoubling, a player should not state the number of odd tricks or the denomination. The only correct form is the single word "Redouble".
   3. Redouble of an Incorrectly Stated Bid

      If a player, in redoubling, incorrectly states the doubled

bid, or the number of odd tricks or the denomination, he is deemed to have redoubled the bid as it was made. (Law 16 – Unauthorized Information – may apply.)

C. Double or Redouble Superseded
Any double or redouble is superseded by a subsequent legal bid.

D. Scoring a Doubled or Redoubled Contract
If a doubled or redoubled bid is not followed by a subsequent legal bid, scoring values are increased as provided in Law 77.

# LAW 20

# REVIEW AND EXPLANATION OF CALLS

A. Call Not Clearly Heard
A player who does not hear a call distinctly may forthwith require that it be repeated.

B. Review of Auction during Auction Period
During the auction period, a player is entitled to have all* previous calls restated when it is his turn to call, unless he is required by law to pass; Alerts should be included in the restatement.

C. Review after Final Pass
  1. Opening Lead Inquiry
     After the final pass either defender has the right to ask if it is his opening lead (see Laws 47E and 41).
  2. Review of Auction
     Declarer or either defender may, at his first turn to play, require all* previous calls to be restated (see Law 41B and 41C).

---

*A player may not ask for a partial restatement of previous calls and may not halt the review before it has been completed.

D. Who May Review the Auction

A request to have calls restated shall be responded to only by an opponent.

E. Correction of Error in Review

All players, including dummy or a player required by law to pass, are responsible for prompt correction of errors in restatement (see Law 12C1 when an uncorrected review causes damage).

F. Explanation of Calls
   1. During the Auction

   During the auction and before the final pass, any player, at his own turn to call, may request* a full explanation of the opponents' auction (questions may be asked about calls actually made or about relevant calls available but not made); replies should normally be given by the partner of a player who made a call in question (see Law 75C).

   2. During the Play Period

   After the final pass and throughout the play period, either defender at his own turn to play may request* an explanation of opposing auction. At his or dummy's turn to play, the declarer may request an explanation of a defender's call or card play conventions.

## LAW 21

## CALL BASED ON MISINFORMATION

A. Call Based on Caller's Misunderstanding

A player has no recourse if he has made a call on the basis of his own misunderstanding.

---

*Law 16 may apply, and sponsoring organizations may establish regulations for written explanation.

B. Call Based on Misinformation from an Opponent
  1. Change of Call
     Until the end of the auction period (see Law 17E), a player may, without penalty, change a call when it is probable that he made the call as a result of misinformation given to him by an opponent (failure to alert promptly to a conventional call or special understanding, where such alert is required by the sponsoring organization, is deemed misinformation), provided that his partner has not subsequently called.
  2. Change of Call by Opponent Following Correction
     When a player elects to change a call because of misinformation (as in 1., preceding), his LHO may then in turn change any subsequent call he may have made, without penalty (unless his withdrawn call conveyed such information as to damage the non-offending side, in which case the Director may assign an adjusted score). (For unauthorized information from withdrawn calls, see Law 16C.)
  3. Too Late to Change Call
     When it is too late to change a call, the Director may award an adjusted score (Law 40C may apply).

## SECTION TWO
## AUCTION HAS ENDED

## LAW 22

## PROCEDURE AFTER THE AUCTION HAS ENDED

After the auction period has ended,
A. No Player Has Bid
   if no player has bid, the hands are returned to the board without play. There shall not be a redeal.

B. One or More Players Have Bid
   if any player has bid, the final bid becomes the contract,
   and play begins.

## PART II
## IRREGULARITIES IN PROCEDURE

## LAW 23

## DAMAGING ENFORCED PASS

Reference will be made to this Law from many other Laws that prescribe penalties for auction-period infractions.

When the penalty for an irregularity under any Law would compel the offender's partner to pass at his next turn, if the Director deems that the offender, at the time of his irregularity, could have known that the enforced pass would be likely to damage the non-offending side, he shall require the auction and play to continue and consider awarding an adjusted score. (See Law 72B1.)

## SECTION ONE
## EXPOSED CARD, AUCTION PERIOD

## LAW 24

## CARD EXPOSED OR LED DURING AUCTION

When the Director determines, during the auction, that because of a player's action one or more cards of that player's hand were in position for the face to be seen by his partner, the Director shall require that every such card be left face up on the table until the auction closes; and (penalty) if the offender subsequently becomes a defender, declarer may treat every such card as a penalty card (Law 50). In addition:

A. Low Card Not Prematurely Led
   If it is a single card below the rank of an honor and not prematurely led, there is no further penalty.

B. Single Card of Honor Rank or Card Prematurely Led
   If it is a single card of honor rank or is any card prematurely led, (penalty) offender's partner must pass when next it is his turn to call (see Law 23 when a pass damages the non-offending side).

C. Two or More Cards Are Exposed
   If two or more cards are so exposed, (penalty) offender's partner must pass when next it is his turn to call (see Law 23 when a pass damages the non-offending side).

## SECTION TWO
## CHANGES OF CALLS

## LAW 25

## LEGAL AND ILLEGAL CHANGES OF CALL

A. Immediate Correction of Inadvertency
   Until his partner makes a call, a player may substitute his intended call for an inadvert call but only if he does so, or attempts to do so, without pause for thought. If legal, his last call stands without penalty; if illegal, it is subject to the applicable Law.

B. Delayed or Purposeful Correction
   Until LHO calls, a call may be substituted when Section

A does not apply:

1. Substitute Call Condoned

   The substituted call may be accepted (treated as legal) at the option of offender's LHO*; then, the second call stands and the auction proceeds without penalty. If offender's LHO has called before attention is drawn to the infraction and the Director determines that LHO intended his call to apply over the offender's original call at that turn, offender's substituted call stands without penalty, and LHO may withdraw his call without penalty (but see Law 16C2).

2. Not Condoned

   If the substituted call is not accepted, it is canceled, and

   (a) First Call Illegal

      if the first call was illegal, the offender is subject to the applicable law (and the lead penalties of Law 26 may apply to the second call).

   (b) First Call Legal

      if the first call was legal, the offender must either

      (1) Let First Call Stand

         allow his first call to stand, in which case (penalty) his partner must pass when next it is his turn to call (see Law 23 when the pass damages the non-offending side), or,

      (2) Substitute Another Call

         make any other legal call, in which case (penalty) the auction proceeds normally (but offender's partner may not base calls on information from withdrawn calls); the offending side** may receive no score greater than average minus (see Law 12C1).

   (c) Lead Penalties

      In either case (b) (1) or (b) (2) above, the offender's

---

*When the original bid was insufficient, apply Law 27.

**The non-offending side receives the score achieved at the table.

partner will be subject to a lead penalty (see Law 26) if he becomes a defender.

## LAW 26

## CALL WITHDRAWN, LEAD PENALTIES

When an offending player's call is withdrawn, and he chooses a different* final call for that turn, then if he becomes a defender:

A. Call Related to Specific Suit
   if the withdrawn call related to a specified suit or suits and
   1. Suit Specified
      if that suit was specified by the same player, there is no lead penalty, but see Law 16C.
   2. Suit Not Specified
      if that suit was not specified in the legal auction by the same player, then declarer may (penalty) either require the offender's partner to lead the specified suit (or one particular specified suit) at his first turn to lead, including the opening lead, or prohibit offender's partner from leading the specified suit (or one particular specified suit) at his first turn to lead, including the opening lead, such prohibition to continue for as long as offender's partner retains the lead.
B. Other Withdrawn Calls
   For other withdrawn calls, (penalty) declarer may prohibit offender's partner from leading any one suit** at his first turn to lead, including the opening lead, such prohibition to continue for as long as offender's partner retains the lead.

---

*A call repeated with a much different meaning shall be deemed a different call.

**Declarer specifies the suit when offender's partner first has the lead.

# SECTION THREE
# INSUFFICIENT BID

## LAW 27

## INSUFFICIENT BID

A. Insufficient Bid Accepted

Any insufficient bid may be accepted (treated as legal) at the option of offender's LHO. It is accepted if that player calls.

B. Insufficient Bid Not Accepted

If an insufficient bid made in rotation is not accepted, it must be corrected by the substitution of either a sufficient bid or a pass.

1. Not Conventional and Corrected by Lowest Sufficient Bid in Same Denomination

   (a) No Penalty

   If both the insufficient bid and the bid substituted are incontrovertibly not conventional and if the bid is corrected by the lowest sufficient bid in the same denomination, the auction proceeds as though the irregularity had not occurred (Law 16C2 does not apply to this situation, but see (b) following).

   (b) Award of Adjusted Score

   If the Director judges that the insufficient bid conveyed such information as to damage the non-offending side, he shall assign an adjusted score.

2. Conventional, or Corrected by Any Other Sufficient Bid or Pass

   If either the insufficient bid or the lowest sufficient bid in the same denomination may have been conventional or if the bid is corrected by any other sufficient bid or by a pass, (penalty) the offender's partner must pass whenever it is his turn to call (apply Law 10C1 and see Law 23 when the pass damages the non-offending side; and the lead penalties of Law 26 may apply).

3. Attempt to Correct by a Double or Redouble
   If the offender attempts to substitute a double or redouble for his insufficient bid, the attempted call is cancelled, and (penalty) his partner must pass whenever it is his turn to call (see Law 23 when the pass damages the non-offending side, and the lead penalties of Law 26 may apply).

C. Insufficient Bid Out of Rotation
   If a player makes an insufficient bid out of rotation, Law 31 applies.

# SECTION FOUR
# CALL OUT OF ROTATION

# LAW 28

## CALLS CONSIDERED TO BE IN ROTATION

A. RHO Required to Pass
   A call is considered to be in rotation when it is made by a player at his RHO's turn to call if that opponent is required by law to pass.

B. Call by Correct Player Cancelling Call Out of Rotation
   A call is considered to be in rotation when made by a player whose turn it was to call, before a penalty has been assessed for a call out of rotation by an opponent; making such a call forfeits the right to penalize the call out of rotation, and the auction proceeds as though the opponent had not called at that turn, but Law 16C2 applies.

# LAW 29

## PROCEDURE AFTER A CALL OUT OF ROTATION

A. Forfeiture of Right to Penalize
   Following a call out of rotation, offender's LHO may elect to call, thereby forfeiting the right to penalize.

B. Out-of-Rotation Call Cancelled
   Otherwise, a call out of rotation is cancelled (but see A preceding), and the auction reverts to the player whose turn it was to call. Offender may make any legal call in proper rotation, but his side may be subject to penalty under Laws 30, 31 or 32.

C. Call Out of Rotation Is Conventional
   If a call out of rotation is conventional, the provisions of Laws 30, 31, and 32 shall apply to the denominations specified, rather than the denominations named.

# LAW 30

## PASS OUT OF ROTATION

When a player has passed out of rotation (and the call is cancelled, as the option to accept the call has not been exercised – see Law 29):

A. Before Any Player Has Bid
   When a player has passed out of rotation before any player has bid, (penalty) the offender must pass when next it is his turn to call and Law 72B1 may apply.

B. After Any Player Has Bid
   1. At RHO's Turn to Call
      After any player has bid, when a pass out of rotation

35

is made at offender's RHO's turn to call, (penalty) offender must pass when next it is his turn to call (if the pass out of rotation related by convention to a specific suit, or suits, thereby conveying information, the lead penalties of Law 26 may apply).

2. At Partner's Turn to Call

    (a) Action Required of Offender

        After any player has bid, for a pass out of rotation made at the offender's partner's turn to call, (penalty) the offender must pass whenever it is his turn to call, and Law 72B1 may apply.

    (b) Action Open to Offender's Partner

        Offender's partner may make any sufficient bid, or may pass, but may not double or redouble at that turn, and Law 72B1 may apply.

3. At LHO's Turn to Call

    After any player has bid, a pass out of rotation at offender's LHO's turn to call is treated as a change of call and Law 25 applies.

C. When Pass Is a Convention

When the pass out of rotation is a convention, Law 31, not this Law, will apply. A pass is a convention if, by special agreement, it promises more than a specified amount of strength, or if it artificially promises or denies values other than in the last suit named.

# LAW 31

## BID OUT OF ROTATION

When a player has bid out of rotation (and the bid is canceled, as the option to accept the bid has not been exercised — see Law 29):

A. RHO's Turn

When the offender has bid (or has passed partner's call when it is a convention, in which case section A2(b) applies) at his RHO's turn to call, then:

1. RHO Passes

   If that opponent passes, offender must repeat the call out of rotation, and when that call is legal there is no penalty.

2. RHO Acts

   If that opponent makes a legal* bid, double or redouble, offender may make any legal call; when this call

   (a) Repeats Denomination

   repeats the denomination of his bid out of rotation, (penalty) offender's partner must pass when next it is his turn to call (see Law 23).

   (b) Does Not Repeat Denomination

   does not repeat the denomination of his bid out of rotation, the lead penalties of Law 26 may apply, and (penalty) offender's partner must pass whenever it is his turn to call (see Law 23).

B. Partner's or LHO's Turn

When the offender has bid at his partner's turn to call, or at his LHO's turn to call if the offender has not previously called,** (penalty) offender's partner must pass whenever it is his turn to call (see Law 23 when the pass damages the non-offending side), and the lead penalties of Law 26 may apply.

---

*An illegal call by RHO is penalized as usual.

**Later bids at LHO's turn to call are treated as changes of call, and Law 25 applies.

# LAW 32

## DOUBLE OR REDOUBLE OUT OF ROTATION

A double or redouble out of rotation may be accepted at the option of the opponent next in rotation (see Law 29), except that an inadmissible double or redouble may never be accepted (see Law 35A if the opponent next in rotation nevertheless does call). If the illegal call is not accepted, it is cancelled, the lead penalties of Law 26B may apply, and:

A. Made at Offender's Partner's Turn to Call
   If a double or redouble out of rotation has been made when it was the offender's partner's turn to call, (penalty) the offender's partner must pass whenever it is his turn to call (see Law 23 when the pass damages the non-offending side).

B. Made at RHO's Turn to Call
   If a double or redouble out of rotation has been made at offender's RHO's turn to call, then:
   1. RHO Passes
      If offender's RHO passes, offender must repeat his out-of-rotation double or redouble and there is no penalty unless the double or redouble is inadmissible, in which case Law 36 applies.
   2. RHO Bids
      If offender's RHO bids, the offender may in turn make any legal call and (penalty) offender's partner must pass whenever it is his turn to call (see Law 23 when the pass damages the non-offending side).

## LAW 33

## SIMULTANEOUS CALLS

A call made simultaneously with one made by the player whose turn it was to call is deemed to be a subsequent call.

## LAW 34

## RETENTION OF RIGHT TO CALL

When a call has been followed by three passes, the auction does not end when one of those passes was out of rotation, thereby depriving a player of his right to call at that turn. The auction reverts to the player who missed his turn. All subsequent passes are cancelled, and the auction proceeds as though there had been no irregularity.

## LAW 35

## INADMISSIBLE CALL CONDONED

When, after any inadmissible call specified below, the offender's LHO makes a call before a penalty has been assessed, there is no penalty for the inadmissible call (the lead penalties of Law 26 do not apply), and:

A. Double or Redouble
   If the inadmissible call was a double or redouble not permitted by Law 19, that call and all subsequent calls are cancelled. The auction reverts to the player whose turn it is to call, and proceeds as though there had been no irregularity.

B. Action by Player Required to Pass
   If the inadmissible call was a bid, double or redouble by a player required by law to pass, that call and all subsequent legal calls stand, but, if the offender was required to pass for the remainder of the auction, he must still pass at subsequent turns.

C. Bid of More than Seven
   If the inadmissible call was a bid of more than seven, that call and all subsequent calls are cancelled; the offender must substitute a pass, and the auction proceeds as though there had been no irregularity.

D. Call after Final Pass
   If the inadmissible call was a call after the final pass of the auction, that call and all subsequent calls are cancelled without penalty.

## SECTION FIVE
## INADMISSIBLE CALLS

## LAW 36

## INADMISSIBLE DOUBLE OR REDOUBLE

Any double or redouble not permitted by Law 19 is cancelled. The offender must substitute a legal call, and (penalty) the offender's partner must pass whenever it is his turn to call (see Law 23 when the pass damages the non-offending side); the lead penalties of Law 26 may apply. (If the call is out of turn, see Law 32; if offender's LHO calls, see Law 35A.)

## LAW 37

### ACTION VIOLATING OBLIGATION TO PASS

A bid, double or redouble by a player who is required by law to pass is cancelled, and (penalty) each member of the offending side must pass whenever it becomes his turn to call (see Law 23 when the pass damages the non-offending side). The lead penalties of Law 26 may apply. (If offender's LHO calls, see Law 35B.)

## LAW 38

### BID OF MORE THAN SEVEN

No play or score at a contract of more than seven is ever permissible. A bid of more than seven is cancelled, and (penalty) each member of the offending side must pass whenever it becomes his turn to call (see Law 23 when the pass damages the non-offending side). The lead penalties of Law 26 may apply. (If offender's LHO calls, see Law 35C.)

## LAW 39

### CALL AFTER FINAL PASS

A call made after the final pass of the auction is cancelled, and:

A. Pass or Call by Declaring Side
   If it is a pass by a defender, or any call by the future declarer or dummy, there is no penalty.

B. Other Action by Defender
If it is a bid, double or redouble by a defender, the lead penalties of Law 26 may apply. (If offender's LHO calls, see Law 35D.)

# SECTION SIX
# CONVENTIONS AND AGREEMENTS

## LAW 40

## PARTNERSHIP UNDERSTANDINGS

A. Right to Choose Call or Play
A player may make any call or play (including an intentionally misleading call – such as a psychic bid – or a call or play that departs from commonly accepted, or previously announced, use of a convention), without prior announcement, provided that such call or play is not based on a partnership understanding.

B. Concealed Partnership Understandings Prohibited
A player may not make a call or play based on a special partnership understanding unless an opposing pair may reasonably be expected to understand its meaning, or unless his side discloses the use of such call or play in accordance with the regulations of the sponsoring organization.

C. Director's Option
If the Director decides that a side has been damaged through its opponents' failure to explain the full meaning of a call or play, he may award an adjusted score.

D. Regulation of Conventions
The sponsoring organization may regulate the use of bidding or play conventions. Zonal organizations may, in

42

addition, regulate partnership understandings (even if not conventional) that permit the partnership's initial actions at the one level to be made with a hand of a King or more below average strength. Zonal organizations may delegate this responsibility.

E. Convention Card
  1. Right to Prescribe
     The sponsoring organization may prescribe a convention card on which partners are to list their conventions and other agreements and may establish regulations for its use, including a requirement that both members of a partnership employ the same system (such a regulation must not restrict style and judgment, only method).
  2. Referring to Opponents' Convention Card
     During the auction and play, any player except dummy may refer to his opponents' convention card at his own turn to call or play, but not to his own*.

---

*A player is not entitled, during the auction and play periods, to any aids to his memory, calculation or technique. However, sponsoring organizations may designate unusual methods and allow written defenses against opponents' unusual methods to be referred to at the table.

# CHAPTER VI

# The Play

## PART I
## PROCEDURE

## SECTION ONE
## CORRECT PROCEDURE

## LAW 41

## COMMENCEMENT OF PLAY

A. Face-down Opening Lead

After a bid, double or redouble has been followed by three passes in rotation, the defender on presumed declarer's left makes the opening lead face down*. The face-down lead may be withdrawn only upon instruction of the Director after an irregularity (see Law 47E2); the withdrawn card must be returned to the defender's hand.

B. Review of Auction and Questions

Before the opening lead is faced, the leader's partner and the presumed declarer each may require a review of the auction, or request explanation of an opponent's call (see Law 20). Declarer or either defender may, at his first turn to play a card, require a review of the auction; this right expires when he plays a card. The defenders (subject to Law 16) and the declarer retain the right to request explanations throughout the play period, each at his own turn to play.

---

* Sponsoring organizations may specify that opening leads be made face up.

C. Opening Lead Faced

Following this question period, the opening lead is faced, the play period begins, and dummy's hand is spread. After it is too late to have previous calls restated (see B, above), declarer or either defender, at his own turn to play, is entitled to be informed as to what the contract is and whether, but not by whom, it was doubled or redoubled.

D. Dummy's Hand

After the opening lead is faced, dummy spreads his hand in front of him on the table, face up, sorted into suits, the cards in order of rank, in columns pointing lengthwise towards declarer, with trumps to dummy's right. Declarer plays both his hand and that of dummy.

# LAW 42

# DUMMY'S RIGHTS

A. Absolute Rights

1. Give Information

Dummy is entitled to give information, in the Director's presence, as to fact or law.

2. Keep Track of Tricks

He may keep count of tricks won and lost.

3. Play as Declarer's Agent

He plays the cards of the dummy as declarer's agent as directed (see Law 45F if dummy suggests a play).

B. Qualified Rights

Dummy may exercise other rights subject to the limitations provided in Law 43.

1. Revoke Inquiries

Dummy may ask declarer (but not a defender) when he has failed to follow suit to a trick whether he has a card of the suit led.

2. Attempt to Prevent Irregularity
   He may try to prevent any irregularity by declarer.

3. Draw Attention to Irregularity
   He may draw attention to any irregularity, but only after play of the hand is concluded.

# LAW 43

## DUMMY'S LIMITATIONS

Except as specified in Law 42:

A. Limitations on Dummy
   1. General Limitations
      (a) Calling the Director
          Unless attention has been drawn to an irregularity by another player, dummy should not initiate a call for the Director during play.
      (b) Calling Attention to Irregularity
          Dummy may not call attention to an irregularity during play.
      (c) Participate in or Comment on Play
          Dummy must not participate in the play, nor may he communicate anything about the play to declarer.
   2. Limitations Carrying Specific Penalty
      (a) Exchanging Hands
          Dummy may not exchange hands with declarer.
      (b) Leave Seat to Watch Declarer
          Dummy may not leave his seat to watch declarer's play of the hand.
      (c) Look at Defender's Hand
          Dummy may not, on his own initiative, look at the face of a card in either defender's hand.

B. Penalties for Violation

   1. General Penalties

     Dummy is liable to penalty under Law 90 for any violation of the limitations listed in A1 or A2 preceding.

   2. Specific Penalties

     If dummy, after violation of the limitations listed in A2 preceding:

     (a) Warns Declarer on Lead

       warns declarer not to lead from the wrong hand, (penalty) either defender may choose the hand from which declarer shall lead.

     (b) Asks Declarer about Possible Irregularity

       is the first to ask declarer if a play from declarer's hand constitutes a revoke, declarer must substitute a correct card if his play was illegal, and the penalty provisions of Law 64 apply as if the revoke had been established.

   3. If dummy after violation of the limitations listed in A2 preceding is the first to draw attention to a defender's irregularity, no penalty shall be imposed. If the defenders benefit directly through their irregularity, the director shall award an adjusted score to both sides to restore equity.

# LAW 44

## SEQUENCE AND PROCEDURE OF PLAY

A. Lead to a Trick

   The player who leads to a trick may play any card in his hand (unless he is subject to restriction after an irregularity committed by his side).

B. Subsequent Plays to a Trick

   After the lead, each other player in turn plays a card, and

the four cards so played constitute a trick. (For the method of playing cards and arranging tricks see Law 65.)

C. Requirement to Follow Suit
   In playing to a trick, each player must follow suit if possible. This obligation takes precedence over all other requirements of these Laws.

D. Inability to Follow Suit
   If unable to follow suit, a player may play any card (unless he is subject to restriction after an irregularity committed by his side).

E. Tricks Containing Trumps
   A trick containing a trump is won by the player who has contributed to it the highest trump.

F. Tricks Not Containing Trumps
   A trick that does not contain a trump is won by the player who has contributed to it the highest card of the suit led.

G. Lead to Tricks Subsequent to First Trick
   The player who has won the trick leads to the next trick.


## LAW 45

## CARD PLAYED

A. Play of Card from a Hand
   Each player except dummy plays a card by detaching it from his hand and facing* it on the table immediately before him.

---

* The opening lead is first made face down (unless the sponsoring organization directs otherwise).

B. Play of Card from Dummy

Declarer plays a card from dummy by naming the card, after which dummy picks up the card and faces it on the table. In playing from dummy's hand declarer may, if necessary, pick up the desired card himself.

C. Compulsory Play of Card

1. Defender's Card

   A defender's card held so that it is possible for his partner to see its face must be played to the current trick (if the defender has already made a legal play to the current trick, see Law 45E).

2. Declarer's Card

   Declarer must play a card from his hand held face up, touching or nearly touching the table, or maintained in such a position as to indicate that it has been played.

3. Dummy's Card

   A card in the dummy must be played if it has been deliberately touched by declarer except for the purpose of arranging dummy's cards, or of reaching a card above or below the card or cards touched.

4. Named or Designated Card

   (a) Play of Named Card

       A card must be played if a player names or otherwise designates it as the card he proposes to play.

   (b) Correction of Inadvertent Designation

       A player may, without penalty, change an inadvertent designation if he does so without pause for thought; but if an opponent has, in turn, played a card that was legal before the change in designation, that opponent may withdraw without penalty the card so played and substitute another (see Law 47E).

5. Penalty Card

   A penalty card, major or minor, may have to be played, subject to Law 50.

D. Card Misplayed by Dummy

If dummy places in the played position a card that declarer did not name, the card must be withdrawn if attention is drawn to it before each side has played to the next trick, and a defender may withdraw (without penalty) a card played after the error but before attention was drawn to it; if declarer's RHO changes his play, declarer may withdraw a card he had subsequently played to that trick (see Law 16C2).

E. Fifth Card Played to Trick
   1. By a Defender
      A fifth card contributed to a trick by a defender becomes a penalty card, subject to Law 50, unless the Director deems that it was led, in which case Law 53 or 56 applies.
   2. By Declarer
      When declarer contributes a fifth card to a trick from his own hand or dummy, there is no penalty unless the Director deems that it was led, in which case Law 55 applies.

F. Dummy Indicates Card

After dummy's hand is faced, dummy may not touch or indicate any card (except for purpose of arrangement) without instruction from declarer. If he does so, the Director should be summoned forthwith. The Director shall rule whether dummy's act did in fact constitute a suggestion to declarer. When the Director judges that it did, he allows play to continue, reserving his right to assign an adjusted score if the defenders were damaged by the play so suggested.

G. Turning the Trick

No player should turn his card face down until all four players have played to the trick.

## SECTION TWO
## IRREGULARITIES IN PROCEDURE

### LAW 46

### INCOMPLETE OR ERRONEOUS CALL OF CARD FROM DUMMY

A. Proper Form for Designating Dummy's Card
   When calling a card to be played from dummy, declarer should clearly state both the suit and the rank of the desired card.

B. Incomplete or Erroneous Call
   In case of an incomplete or erroneous call by declarer of the card to be played from dummy, the following restrictions apply (except when declarer's different intention is incontrovertible):
   1. Incomplete Designation of Rank
      If declarer, in playing from dummy, calls "high", or words of like import, he is deemed to have called the highest card: in fourth seat he may be deemed to have called for the lowest winning card of the suit indicated; if he directs dummy to win the trick, he is deemed to have called the lowest winning card; if he calls "low", or words of like import, he is deemed to have called the lowest.
   2. Designates Suit but Not Rank
      If declarer designates a suit but not a rank, he is deemed to have called the lowest card of the suit indicated.
   3. Designates Rank but Not Suit
      If declarer designates a rank but not a suit:
      (a) In Leading
          Declarer is deemed to have continued the suit in which dummy won the preceding trick, provided there is a card of the designated rank in that suit.

(b) All Other Cases

In all other cases, declarer must play a card from dummy of the designated rank if he can legally do so; but if there are two or more such cards that can be legally played, declarer must designate which is intended.

4. Designates Card Not in Dummy

If declarer calls a card that is not in dummy, the call is void and declarer may designate any legal card.

5. No Suit or Rank Designated

If declarer indicates a play without designating either a suit or rank (as by saying, ""play anything", or words of like import), either defender may designate the play from dummy.

## LAW 47

## RETRACTION OF CARD PLAYED

A. To Comply with Penalty

A card once played may be withdrawn to comply with a penalty (but a defender's withdrawn card may become a penalty card, see Law 49).

B. To Correct an Illegal Play

A played card may be withdrawn to correct an illegal or simultaneous play (see Law 58 for simultaneous play; and, for defenders, see Law 49, penalty card).

C. To Change an Inadvertent Designation

A played card may be withdrawn without penalty after a change of designation as permitted by Law 45C4(b).

D. Following Opponent's Change of Play

After an opponent's change of play, a played card may be

withdrawn without penalty (but see 62C2) to substitute
another card for the one played.

E. Change of Play Based on Misinformation
  1. Lead Out of Turn
    A lead out of turn may be retracted without penalty if
    the leader was mistakenly informed by an opponent that
    it was his turn to lead (LHO should not accept the lead).
  2. Retraction of Play
    (a) No One Has Subsequently Played
      A player may retract the card he has played be-
      cause of a mistaken explanation of an opponent's
      call or play and before a corrected explanation,
      but only if no card was subsequently played to
      that trick. An opening lead may not be retracted
      after dummy has faced any card.
    (b) One or More Subsequent Plays Made
      When it is too late to correct a play, under (a)
      preceding, Law 40C applies.

F. Illegal Retraction
  Except as provided in A through E preceding, a card once
  played may not be withdrawn.

# PART II
# PENALTY CARD

# LAW 48

# EXPOSURE OF DECLARER'S CARDS

A. Declarer Exposes a Card
  Declarer is not subject to penalty for exposing a card,
  and no card of declarer's or dummy's hand ever becomes
  a penalty card. Declarer is not required to play any card

dropped accidentally.
B. Declarer Faces Cards
  1. After Opening Lead Out of Turn
     When declarer faces his cards after an opening lead
     out of turn, Law 54 applies.
  2. At Any Other Time
     When declarer faces his cards at any time other than
     immediately after an opening lead out of turn, he may
     be deemed to have made a claim or concession of tricks,
     and Law 68 then applies.

# LAW 49

## EXPOSURE OF A DEFENDER'S CARDS

Except in the normal course of play or application of law,
when a defender's card is in a position in which his partner
could possibly see its face, or when a defender names a card
as being in his hand, (penalty) each such card becomes a
penalty card (Law 50); but see the footnote to Law 68 when
a defender has made a statement concerning an uncompleted
trick currently in progress.

# LAW 50

## DISPOSITION OF PENALTY CARD

A card prematurely exposed (but not led, see Law 57) by
a defender is a penalty card unless the Director designates
otherwise. The Director shall award an adjusted score, in
lieu of the rectifications below, when he deems that Law
72B1 applies.

A. Penalty Card Remains Exposed

A penalty card must be left face up on the table immediately before the player to whom it belongs, until an alternate penalty has been selected.

B. Major or Minor Penalty Card?

A single card below the rank of an honor and exposed inadvertently (as in playing two cards to a trick, or in dropping a card accidentally) becomes a minor penalty card. Any card of honor rank, or any card exposed through deliberate play (as in leading out of turn, or in revoking and then correcting), becomes a major penalty card; when one defender has two or more penalty cards, all such cards become major penalty cards.

C. Disposition of Minor Penalty Card

When a defender has a minor penalty card, he may not play any other card of the same suit below the rank of an honor until he has first played the penalty card (however, he is entitled to play an honor card instead). Offender's partner is not subject to lead penalty, but information gained through seeing the penalty card is extraneous, unauthorized (see Law 16A).

D. Disposition of Major Penalty Card

When a defender has a major penalty card, both the offender and his partner may be subject to restriction, the offender whenever he is to play, the partner when he is to lead.

1. Offender to Play

A major penalty card must be played at the first legal opportunity, whether in leading, following suit, discarding or trumping (the requirement that offender must play the card is authorized information for his partner; however, other information arising from facing of the penalty card is unauthorized for partner). If a defender has two or more penalty cards that can legally be played, declarer designates which is to be a lead or play penalty, takes precedence over the obligation to play a major penalty card, but the penalty card must still be left face up on the table and played at the next legal opportunity.

2. Offender's Partner to Lead

When a defender has the lead while his partner has a major penalty card, he may not lead until declarer has stated which of the options below is selected (if the defender leads prematurely, he is subject to penalty under Law 49). Declarer may choose:

(a) Require or Forbid Lead of Suit

to require* the defender to lead the suit of the penalty card, or to prohibit* him from leading that suit for as long as he retains the lead (for two or more penalty cards, see Law 51); if declarer exercises this option, the card is no longer a penalty card and is picked up.

(b) No Lead Restriction

not to require or prohibit a lead, in which case the defender may lead any card; the penalty card remains a penalty card.

# LAW 51

## TWO OR MORE PENALTY CARDS

A. Offender to Play

If a defender has two or more penalty cards that can legally be played, declarer designates which is to be played at that turn.

B. Offender's Partner to Lead

---

* If the player is unable to lead as required, see Law 59.

1. Penalty Cards in Same Suit
   (a) Declarer Requires Lead of That Suit
       When a defender has two or more penalty cards in one suit, and declarer requires the defender's partner to lead that suit, the cards of that suit are no longer penalty cards and are picked up; the defender may make any legal play to the trick.
   (b) Declarer Prohibits Lead of That Suit
       If the declarer prohibits the lead of that suit, the defender picks up every penalty card in that suit and may make any legal play to the trick.
2. Penalty Cards in More Than One Suit
   (a) Declarer Requires Lead of a Specified Suit
       When a defender has penalty cards in more than one suit, declarer may require* the defender's partner to lead any suit in which the defender has a penalty card (but B1(a) preceding then applies).
   (b) Declarer Prohibits Lead of Specified Suits
       When a defender has penalty cards in more than one suit, declarer may prohibit* the defender's partner from leading one or more of such suits; but the defender then picks up every penalty card in every suit prohibited by declarer and makes any legal play to the trick.

---

* If the player is unable to lead as required, see Law 59.

# LAW 52

## FAILURE TO LEAD OR PLAY A PENALTY CARD

A. Defender Fails to Play Penalty Card
When a defender fails to lead or play a penalty card as required by Law 50, he may not, on his own initiative, withdraw any other card he has played.

B. Defender Plays Another Card
  1. Play of Card Accepted
     (a) Declarer May Accept Play
        If a defender has led or played another card when required by law to play a penalty card, declarer may accept such lead or play.
     (b) Declarer Must Accept Play
        Declarer must accept such lead or play if he has thereafter played from his own hand or dummy.
     (c) Penalty Card Remains Penalty Card
        If the played card is accepted under either (a) or (b) preceding, the unplayed penalty card remains a penalty card.
  2. Play of Card Rejected
     Declarer may require the defender to substitute the penalty card for the card illegally played or led. Every card illegally led or played by the defender in the course of committing the irregularity becomes a major penalty card.

# PART III
# IRREGULAR LEADS AND PLAYS

## SECTION ONE
## LEAD OUT OF TURN

### LAW 53

### LEAD OUT OF TURN ACCEPTED

A. Lead Out of Turn Treated as Correct Lead
   Any lead faced out of turn may be treated as a correct lead. It becomes a correct lead if declarer or either defender, as the case may be, accepts it (by making a statement to that effect), or if the player next in rotation plays* to the irregular lead, but see Law 47E1. (If no acceptance statement or play is made, the Director will require that the lead be made from the correct hand.)

B. Wrong Defender Plays Card to Declarer's Irregular Lead
   If the defender at the right of the hand from which the lead out of turn was made plays* to the irregular lead, the lead stands and Law 57 applies.

C. Proper Lead Made Subsequent to Irregular Lead
   If it was properly the turn to lead of an opponent of the player who led out of turn, that opponent may make his proper lead to the trick of the infraction without his card being deemed played to the irregular lead. When this occurs, the proper lead stands, and all cards played in error to this trick may be withdrawn without penalty. (Law 16C2 applies to a defender.)

---

\* But see C below.

# LAW 54

# FACED OPENING LEAD OUT OF TURN

When an opening lead is faced out of turn, and offender's partner leads face down, the director requires the face down lead to be retracted, and the following sections apply.

A. Declarer Spreads His Hand

After a faced opening lead out of turn, declarer may spread his hand; he becomes dummy, and dummy becomes declarer. If declarer begins to spread his hand, and in doing so exposes one or more cards, he must spread his entire hand.

B. Declarer Accepts Lead

When a defender faces the opening lead out of turn declarer may accept the irregular lead as provided in Law 53, and dummy is spread in accordance with Law 41.

1. Declarer Plays Second Card

The second card to the trick is played from declarer's hand.

2. Dummy Has Played Second Card

If declarer plays the second card to the trick from dummy, dummy's card may not be withdrawn except to correct a revoke.

C. Declarer Must Accept Lead

If declarer could have seen any of dummy's cards (except cards that dummy may have exposed during the auction and that were subject to Law 24), he must accept the lead.

D. Declarer Refuses Opening Lead

When declarer requires the defender to retract his faced opening lead out of turn, Law 56 applies.

# LAW 55

## DECLARER'S LEAD OUT OF TURN

A. Declarer's Lead Accepted
   If declarer has led out of turn from his or dummy's hand, either defender may accept the lead as provided in Law 53, or require its retraction (after misinformation, see Law 47E1).

B. Declarer Required to Retract Lead
   1. Defender's Turn to Lead
      If declarer has led from his or dummy's hand when it was a defender's turn to lead, and if either defender requires him to retract such lead, declarer restores the card led in error to the proper hand without penalty.
   2. Lead in Declarer's Hand or Dummy's
      If declarer has led from the wrong hand when it was his turn to lead from his hand or dummy's, and if either defender requires him to retract the lead, he withdraws the card led in error. He must lead from the correct hand.

C. Declarer Might Obtain Information
   When declarer adopts a line of play that could have been based on information obtained through the infraction, the Director may award an adjusted score.

# LAW 56

## DEFENDER'S LEAD OUT OF TURN

When declarer requires a defender to retract his faced lead out of turn, the card illegally led becomes a major penalty card, and Law 50D applies.

## SECTION TWO
## OTHER IRREGULAR LEADS AND PLAYS

## LAW 57

### PREMATURE LEAD OR PLAY BY DEFENDER

A. Premature Play or Lead to Next Trick
   When a defender leads to the next trick before his partner has played to the current trick, or plays out of turn
   before his partner has played, (penalty) the card so led or
   played becomes a penalty card, and declarer selects one
   of the following options. He may:
   1. Highest Card
      require offender's partner to play the highest card he
      holds of the suit led, or
   2. Lowest Card
      require offender's partner to play the lowest card he
      holds of the suit led, or
   3. Card of Another Suit
      forbid offender's partner to play a card of another suit
      specified by declarer.

B. Offender's Partner Cannot Comply with Penalty
   When offender's partner is unable to comply with the
   penalty selected by declarer, he may play any card, as
   provided in Law 59.

C. Declarer Has Played from Both Hands before Irregularity
   A defender is not subject to penalty for playing before
   his partner if declarer has played from both hands, or if
   dummy has played a card or has illegally suggested that
   it be played. A singleton in dummy, or one of cards adja-

cent in rank of the same suit, is not considered to be automatically played.

# LAW 58

## SIMULTANEOUS LEADS OR PLAYS

A. Simultaneous Plays by Two Players
   A lead or play made simultaneously with another player's legal lead or play is deemed to be subsequent to it.

B. Simultaneous Cards from One Hand
   If a player leads or plays two or more cards simultaneously:
   1. One Card Visible
      If only one card is visible, that card is played; all other cards are picked up without penalty.
   2. More Cards Visible
      If more than one card is visible, the player designates the card he proposes to play; when he is a defender, each other card exposed becomes a penalty card (see Law 50).
   3. After Visible Card Withdrawn
      After a player withdraws a visible card, an opponent who subsequently played to that card may withdraw his play and substitute another without penalty (see Law 16C).
   4. Error Not Discovered
      If the simultaneous play remains undiscovered until both sides have played to the next trick, Law 67 applies.

# LAW 59

## INABILITY TO LEAD OR PLAY AS REQUIRED

A player may play any otherwise legal card if he is unable to lead or play as required to comply with a penalty, whether because he holds no card of the required suit, or because he has only cards of a suit he is prohibited from leading, or because he is obliged to follow suit.

# LAW 60

## PLAY AFTER AN ILLEGAL PLAY

A. Play of Card after Irregularity
  1. Forfeiture of Right to Penalize
     A play by a member of the non-offending side after his RHO has led or played out of turn or prematurely, and before a penalty has been assessed, forfeits the right to penalize that offense.
  2. Irregularity Legalized
     Once the right to penalize has been forfeited, the illegal play is treated as though it were in turn (but Law 53C applies to the player whose turn it was).
  3. Other Penalty Obligations Remain
     If the offending side has a previous obligation to play a penalty card, or to comply with a lead or play penalty, the obligation remains at future turns.

B. Defender Plays before Required Lead by Declarer
   When a defender plays a card after declarer has been required to retract his lead out of turn from either hand, but before declarer has led from the correct hand, the defender's card becomes a penalty card (Law 50).

C. Play by Offending Side before Assessment of Penalty
   A play by a member of the offending side before a penalty has been assessed does not affect the rights of the opponents, and may itself be subject to penalty.

## SECTION THREE
## THE REVOKE

### LAW 61

### FAILURE TO FOLLOW SUIT—
### INQUIRIES CONCERNING A REVOKE

A. Definition of Revoke
   Failure to follow suit in accordance with Law 44 or failure to lead or play, when able, a card or suit required by law or specified by an opponent in accordance with an agreed penalty, constitutes a revoke (but see Law 59 when unable to comply).

B. Right to Inquire about a Possible Revoke
   Declarer may ask a defender who has failed to follow suit whether he has a card of the suit led (but a claim of revoke does not automatically warrant inspection of quitted tricks — see Law 66C). Dummy may ask declarer (but see Law 43B2(b)). Defenders may ask declarer but, unless the zonal organization so authorizes, not one another.

   *NOTE:* *The ACBL Board of Directors under the authority granted in the revised Law 61B, has ruled that in ACBL sanctioned events, a defender may inquire of his partner whether he has a card of the suit led.*

### LAW 62

### CORRECTION OF A REVOKE

A. Revoke Must Be Corrected

A player must correct his revoke if he becomes aware of the irregularity before it becomes established.

B. Correcting a Revoke
   To correct a revoke, the offender withdraws the card he played in revoking and follows suit with any card.
   1. Defender's Card
      A card so withdrawn becomes a penalty card (Law 50) if it was played from a defender's unfaced hand.
   2. Declarer's or Dummy's Card, Defender's Faced Card
      The card may be replaced without penalty if it was played from declarer's or dummy's hand*, or if it was a defender's faced card.

C. Subsequent Cards Played to Trick
   1. By Non-offending Side
      Each member of the non-offending side may, without penalty, withdraw any card he may have played after the revoke but before attention was drawn to it (see Law 16C).
   2. By Partner of Offender
      After a non-offender so withdraws a card, the hand of the offending side next in rotation may withdraw its played card, which becomes a penalty card if the player is a defender (see Law 16C).

D. Revoke on Trick Twelve
   1. Must Be Corrected
      On the twelfth trick, a revoke, even if established, must be corrected if discovered before all four hands have been returned to the board.
   2. Offender's Partner Had Not Played to Trick Twelve
      If a revoke by a defender occurred before it was the

---

* Subject to Law 43B2(b), when dummy has forfeited his rights. A claim of revoke does not warrant inspection of quitted tricks except as permitted in Law 66C.

turn of his partner to play to the twelfth trick, and if offender's partner has cards of two suits, (penalty) offender's partner may not choose the play that could possibly have been suggested by seeing the revoke card.

# LAW 63

## ESTABLISHMENT OF A REVOKE

A. Revoke Becomes Established

A revoke becomes established:

1. Offending Side Leads or Plays to Next Trick
when the offender or his partner leads or plays to the following trick (any such play, legal or illegal, establishes the revoke).

2. A Member of Offending Side Indicates a Lead or Play
when the offender or his partner names or otherwise designates a card to be played to the following trick.

3. Member of Offending Side Makes a Claim or Concession
when a member of the offending side makes or acquiesces in a claim or concession of tricks orally or by facing his hand (or in any other fashion).

B. Attention Is Illegally Drawn

When there has been a violation of Law 61B, the revoker must substitute a legal card and the penalty provisions of Law 64 apply as if the revoke had been established.

C. Revoke May Not Be Corrected

Once a revoke is established, it may no longer be corrected (except as provided in Law 62D for a revoke on the twelfth trick), and the trick on which the revoke occurred stands as played (but see Law 43B2(b)).

# LAW 64

## PROCEDURE AFTER ESTABLISHMENT OF A REVOKE

A. Penalty Assessed

When a revoke is established:

1. Offending Player Won Revoke Trick

   and the trick on which the revoke occurred was won by the offending player, (penalty) after play ceases, the trick on which the revoke occurred plus one of any subsequent tricks won by the offending side are transferred to the non-offending side.

2. Offending Player Did Not Win Revoke Trick

   and the trick on which the revoke occurred was not won by the offending player, then, if the offending side won that or any subsequent trick, (penalty) after play ceases, one trick is transferred to the non-offending side; also, if an additional trick was subsequently won by the offending player with a card that he could legally have played to the revoke trick, one such trick is transferred to the non-offending side.

B. No Penalty Assessed

The penalty for an established revoke does not apply:

1. Offending Side Fails to Win Revoke Trick or Subsequent Trick

   if the offending side did not win either the revoke trick or any subsequent trick.

2. Second Revoke in Same Suit by Offender

   to a subsequent revoke in the same suit by the same player.

3. Revoke by Failure to Play a Faced Card

   if the revoke was made in failing to play any card faced on the table or belonging to a hand faced on the table, including a card from dummy's hand.

4. After Non-offending Side Calls to Next Deal

      if attention was first drawn to the revoke after a member of the non-offending side has made a call on the subsequent deal.

  5. After Round Has Ended
     if attention was first drawn to the revoke after the round has ended.

  6. Revoke on Twelfth Trick
     to a revoke on the twelfth trick.

C. Director Responsible for Equity
  When, after any established revoke, including those not subject to penalty, the Director deems that the non-offending side is insufficiently compensated by this Law for the damage caused, he shall assign an adjusted score.

## PART IV
## TRICKS

## LAW 65

## ARRANGEMENT OF TRICKS

A. Completed Trick
  When four cards have been played to a trick, each player turns his own card face down near him on the table.

B. Keeping Track of the Ownership of Tricks
  1. Tricks Won
     If the player's side has won the trick, the card is pointed lengthwise toward his partner.
  2. Tricks Lost
     If the opponents have won the trick, the card is pointed lengthwise toward the opponents.

C. Orderliness

Each player arranges his own cards in an orderly overlapping row in the sequence played, so as to permit review of the play after its completion, if necessary to determine the number of tricks won by each side or the order in which the cards were played.

D. Agreement on Results of Play

A player should not disturb the order of his played cards until agreement has been reached on the number of tricks won. A player who fails to comply with the provisions of this Law jeopardizes his right to claim ownership of doubtful tricks or to claim a revoke.

# LAW 66

## INSPECTION OF TRICKS

A. Current Trick

So long as his side has not led or played to the next trick, declarer or either defender may, until he has turned his own card face down on the table, require that all cards just played to the trick be faced.

B. Own Last Card

Until a card is led to the next trick, declarer or either defender may inspect, but not expose, his own last card played.

C. Quitted Tricks

Thereafter, until play ceases, quitted tricks may not be inspected (except at the Director's specific instruction; for example, to verify a claim of a revoke).

D. After the Conclusion of Play

After play ceases, the played and unplayed cards may be inspected to settle a claim of a revoke, or of the number of tricks won or lost; but no player should handle cards other than his own. If, after such a claim has been made, a player mixes his cards in such a manner that the Director can no longer ascertain the facts, the Director shall rule in favor of the other side.

# LAW 67

## DEFECTIVE TRICK

A. Before Both Sides Play to Next Trick
   When a player has omitted to play to a trick, or has played too many cards to a trick, the error must be rectified if attention is drawn to the irregularity before a player on each side has played to the following trick.
   1. Player Failed to Play Card
      To rectify omission to play to a trick, the offender supplies a card he can legally play.
   2. Player Contributed Too Many Cards
      To rectify the play of too many cards to a trick, Law 45E (Fifth Card Played to a Trick) or Law 58B (Simultaneous Cards from One Hand) shall be applied.

B. After Both Sides Play to Next Trick
   After both sides have played to the following trick, when attention is drawn to a defective trick or when the Director determines that there had been a defective trick (from the fact that one player has too few or too many cards in his hand, and a correspondingly incorrect number of played cards), the Director establishes which trick was defective. To rectify the number of cards, the Director should proceed as follows.
   1. Offender Has Too Many Cards

When the offender has failed to play a card to the defective trick, the Director shall require him forthwith to face a card and to place it appropriately among his played cards (this card does not affect ownership of the trick); if

(a) Offender Has Card of Suit Led

the offender has a card of the suit led to the defective trick, he must choose such a card to place among his played cards, and there is no penalty.

(b) Offender Has No Card of Suit Led

the offender has no card of the suit led to the defective trick, he chooses any card to place among his played cards, and (penalty) he is deemed to have revoked on the defective trick — he may be subject to the one-trick penalty of Law 64.

2. Offender Has Too Few Cards

When the offender has played more than one card to the defective trick, the Director inspects the played cards and requires the offender to restore to his hand all extra cards*, leaving among the played cards the one faced in playing to the defective trick (if the Director is unable to determine which card was faced, the offender leaves the highest of the cards that he could legally have played to the trick). A restored card is deemed to have belonged continuously to the offender's hand, and a failure to have played it to an earlier trick may constitute a revoke.

---

* The Director should avoid, when possible, exposing a defender's played cards, but if an extra card to be restored to a defender's hand has been exposed, it becomes a penalty card (see Law 50).

## PART V
## CLAIMS AND CONCESSIONS

## LAW 68

### CLAIM OR CONCESSION OF TRICKS

For a statement or action to constitute a claim or concession of tricks under these Laws, it must refer to tricks other than one currently in progress*. If it does refer to subsequent tricks:

A. Claim Defined

Any statement to the effect that a contestant will win a specific number of tricks is a claim of those tricks. A contestant also claims when he suggests that play be curtailed, or when he shows his cards (unless he demonstrably did not intend to claim).

B. Concession Defined

Any statement to the effect that a contestant will lose a specific number of tricks is a concession of those tricks; a claim of some number of tricks is a concession of the remainder, if any. A player concedes all the remaining tricks when he abandons his hand. Regardless of the foregoing, if a defender attempts to concede one or more tricks and his partner immediately objects, no concession has occurred; Law 16, Unauthorized Information, may apply, so the Director should be summoned forthwith.

---

* If the statement or action pertains only to the winning or losing of an uncompleted trick currently in progress, play proceeds regularly; cards exposed or revealed by a defender do not become penalty cards, but Law 16, Unauthorized Information, may apply, and see Law 57A, Premature Play.

C. Clarification Required for Claim

A claim should be accompanied at once by a statement of clarification as to the order in which cards will be played, the line of play or defense through which the claimer proposes to win the tricks claimed.

D. Play Ceases

After any claim or concession, play ceases. All play subsequent to a claim or concession shall be voided by the Director. If the claim or concession is acquiesced in, Law 69 applies; if it is disputed by any player (dummy included), the Director must be summoned immediately to apply Law 70 or Law 71, and no action may be taken pending the Director's arrival.

# LAW 69

## ACQUIESCENCE IN CLAIM OR CONCESSION

A. When Acquiescence Occurs

Acquiescence occurs when a contestant assents to an opponent's claim or concession, and raises no objection to it before his side makes a call on a subsequent board, or before the round ends. The board is scored as though the tricks claimed or conceded had been won or lost in play.

B. Acquiescence in Claim Withdrawn

Within the correction period established in accordance with Law 79C, a contestant may withdraw aquiescence in an opponent's claim, but only if he has acquiesced in the loss of a trick his side has actually won, or in the loss of trick that could not, in the Director's judgment, be lost by any normal* play of the remaining cards. The board is rescored with such trick awarded to the acquiescing side.

---

* For the purposes of Laws 69, 70 and 71, "normal" includes play that would be careless or inferior for the class of player involved, but not irrational.

# LAW 70

# CONTESTED CLAIMS

A. General Objective

In ruling on a contested claim, the Director adjudicates the result of the board as equitably as possible to both sides, but any doubtful points shall be resolved against the claimer. The Director proceeds as follows.

B. Clarification Statement Repeated

1. Require Claimer to Repeat Statement

The Director requires claimer to repeat the clarification statement he made at the time of his claim.

2. Require All Hands to Be Faced

Next, the Director requires all players to put their remaining cards face up on the table.

3. Hear Objections

The Director then hears the opponents' objections to the claim.

C. There Is an Outstanding Trump

When a trump remains in one of the opponents' hands, the Director shall award a trick or tricks to the opponents if:

1. Failed to Mention Trump

claimer made no statement about that trump, and

2. Was Probably Unaware of Trump

it is at all likely that claimer at the time of his claim was unaware that a trump remained in an opponent's hand, and

3. Could Lose a Trick to the Trump

a trick could be lost to that trump by any normal* play.

---

* For the purposes of Laws 69, 70 and 71, "normal" includes play that would be careless or inferior for the class of player involved, but not irrational.

D. Claimer Proposes New Line of Play

The Director shall not accept from claimer any successful line of play not embraced in the original clarification statement if there is an alternative normal* line of play that would be less successful.

E. Unstated Line of Play (Finesse or Drop)

The Director shall not accept from claimer any unstated line of play the success of which depends upon finding one opponent rather than the other with a particular card, unless an opponent failed to follow to the suit of that card before the claim was made, or would subsequently fail to follow to that suit on any normal* line of play; or unless failure to adopt this line of play would be irrational.

# LAW 71

## CONCESSION CANCELED

A concession must stand, once made, except that within the correction period established in accordance with Law 79C, the Director shall cancel a concession:

A. Trick Cannot Be Lost

if a player has conceded a trick his side had, in fact, won, or a trick his side could not have lost by any legal play of the remaining cards.

---

* For the purposes of Laws 69, 70 and 71, "normal" includes play that would be careless or inferior for the class of player involved, but not irrational.

B. Contract Already Fulfilled or Defeated
   if declarer has conceded defeat of a contract he had already fulfilled, or a defender has conceded fulfillment of a contract his side had already defeated.

C. Implausible Concession
   if a player has conceded a trick that cannot be lost by any normal* play of the remaining cards. Until the conceding side makes a call on a subsequent board, or until the round ends, the Director shall cancel the concession of a trick that could not have been lost by any normal* play of the remaining cards.

---

* For the purposes of Laws 69, 70 and 71, "normal" includes play that would be careless or inferior for the class of player involved, but not irrational.

# CHAPTER VII

# **Proprieties**

## LAW 72

## GENERAL PRINCIPLES

A. Observance of Laws
1. General Obligation on Contestants
   Duplicate bridge tournaments should be played in strict accordance with the Laws.
2. Scoring of Tricks Won
   A player must not knowingly accept either the score for a trick that his side did not win or the concession of a trick that his opponents could not lose.
3. Waiving of Penalties
   In duplicate tournaments a player may not, on his own initiative, waive a penalty for an opponent's infraction, even if he feels that he has not been damaged (but he may ask the Director to do so — see Law 81C8).
4. Non-offenders' Exercise of Legal Options
   When these Laws provide the innocent side with an option after an irregularity committed by an opponent, it is appropriate to select that action most advantageous.
5. Offenders' Options
   Subject to Law 16C2, after the offending side has paid the prescribed penalty for an inadvertent infraction, it is appropriate for the offenders to make any call or play advantageous to their side, even though they thereby appear to profit through their own infraction.
6. Responsibility for Enforcement of Laws
   The responsibility for penalizing irregularities and redressing damage rests solely upon the Director and these Laws, not upon the players themselves.

B. Infraction of Law
  1. Adjusted Score
     Whenever the Director deems that an offender could have known at the time of his irregularity that the irregularity would be likely to damage the non-offending side, he shall require the auction and play to continue, afterwards awarding an adjusted score if he considers that the offending side gained an advantage through the irregularity.
  2. Intentional
     A player must not infringe a law intentionally, even if there is a prescribed penalty he is willing to pay.
  3. Inadvertent Infraction
     There is no obligation to draw attention to an inadvertent infraction of law committed by one's own side (but see footnote to Law 75 for a mistaken explanation).
  4. Concealing an Infraction
     A player may not attempt to conceal an inadvertent infraction, as by committing a second revoke, concealing a card involved in a revoke or mixing the cards prematurely.

# LAW 73

## COMMUNICATION

A. Proper Communication between Partners
  1. How Effected
     Communication between partners during the auction and play shall be effected only by means of the calls and plays themselves.
  2. Correct Manner for Calls and Plays
     Calls and plays should be made without special emphasis, mannerism or inflection, and without undue

hesitation or haste (however, sponsoring organizations may require mandatory pauses, as on the first round of auction, or after a skip-bid warning, or on the first trick).

B. Inappropriate Communication Between Partners
   1. Gratuitous Information
      Partners shall not communicate through the manner in which calls or plays are made, through extraneous remarks or gestures, through questions asked or not asked of the opponents or through alerts and explanations given or not given to them.
   2. Prearranged Communication
      The gravest possible offense is for a partnership to exchange information through prearranged methods of communication other than those sanctioned by these Laws. A guilty partnership risks expulsion.

C. Player Receives Unauthorized Information from Partner
   When a player has available to him unauthorized information from his partner, as from a remark, question, explanation, gesture, mannerism, special emphasis, inflection, haste or hesitation, he must carefully avoid taking any advantage that might accrue to his side.

D. Variations in Tempo or Manner
   1. Inadvertent Variations
      It is desirable, though not always required, for players to maintain steady tempo and unvarying manner. However, players should be particularly careful in positions in which variations may work to the benefit of their side. Otherwise, inadvertently to vary the tempo or manner in which a call or play is made does not in itself constitute a violation of propriety, but inferences from such variation may appropriately be drawn only by an opponent, and at his own risk.
   2. Intentional Variations
      A player may not attempt to mislead an opponent by

means of remark or gesture, through the haste or hesitancy of a call or play (as in hesitating before playing a singleton), or by the manner in which the call or play is made.

E. Deception

A player may appropriately attempt to deceive an opponent through a call or play (so long as the deception is not protected by concealed partnership understanding or experience). It is entirely appropriate to avoid giving information to the opponents by making all calls and plays in unvarying tempo and manner.

F. Violation of Proprieties

When a violation of the Proprieties described in this law results in damage to an innocent opponent,

1.  Player Acts on Unauthorized Information

    if the Director determines that a player chose from among logical alternative actions one that could demonstrably have been suggested over another by his partner's remark, manner, tempo, or the like, he shall award an adjusted score (see Law 16).

2.  Player Injured by Illegal Deception

    if the Director determines that an innocent player has drawn a false inference from a remark, manner, tempo, or the like, of an opponent who has no demonstrable bridge reason for the action, and who could have known, at the time of the action, that the action could work to his benefit, the Director shall award an adjusted score (see Law 12C),

# LAW 74

## CONDUCT AND ETIQUETTE

A. Proper Attitude
1. Courtesy
A player should maintain a courteous attitude at all times .
2. Etiquette of Word and Action
A player should carefully avoid any remark or action that might cause annoyance or embarrassment to another player or might interfere with the enjoyment of the game.
3. Conformity to Correct Procedure
Every player should follow uniform and correct procedure in calling and playing.

B. Etiquette
As a matter of courtesy a player should refrain from:
1. paying insufficient attention to the game.
2. making gratuitous comments during the auction and play.
3. detaching a card before it is his turn to play.
4. prolonging play unnecessarily (as in playing on although he knows that all the tricks are surely his) for the purpose of disconcerting an opponent.
5. summoning and addressing the Director in a manner discourteous to him or to other contestants.

C. Violations of Procedure
The following are considered violations of procedure:
1. using different designations for the same call.
2. indicating approval or disapproval of a call or play.
3. indicating the expectation or intention of winning or losing a trick that has not been completed.
4. commenting or acting during the auction or play so

as to call attention to a significant occurrence, or to the number of tricks still required for success.

5. looking intently at any other player during the auction and play, or at another player's hand as for the purpose of seeing his cards or of observing the place from which he draws a card (but it is appropriate to act on information acquired by inadvertently seeing an opponent's card*).

6. showing an obvious lack of further interest in a deal (as by folding one's cards).

7. varying the normal tempo of bidding or play for the purpose of disconcerting an opponent.

8. leaving the table needlessly before the round is called.

## LAW 75

## PARTNERSHIP AGREEMENTS

A. Special Partnership Agreements
Special partnership agreements, whether explicit or implicit, must be fully and freely available to the opponents (see Law 40). Information conveyed to partner through such agreements must arise from the calls, plays and conditions of the current deal.

B. Violations of Partnership Agreements
A player may violate an announced partnership agreement, so long as his partner is unaware of the violation (but habitual violations within a partnership may create implicit agreements, which must be disclosed). No player has the obligation to disclose to the opponents that he has violated an announced agreement and if the opponents are subsequently damaged, as through drawing a

---

*See Law 73D2 when a player may have shown his cards intentionally.

false inference from such violation, they are not entitled to redress.

C. Answering Questions on Partnership Agreements
When explaining the significance of partner's call or play in reply to an opponent's inquiry (see Law 20), a player shall disclose all special information conveyed to him through partnership agreement or partnership experience, but he need not disclose inferences drawn from his general knowledge and experience.

D. Correcting Errors in Explanation
1. Explainer Notices Own Error
If a player subsequently realizes that his own explanation was erroneous or incomplete, he must immediately call the Director (who will apply Law 21 or Law 40C).

2. Error Noticed by Explainer's Partner
A player whose partner has given a mistaken explanation may not correct the error before the final pass, nor may he indicate in any manner that a mistake has been made; a defender may not correct the error until play ends. After calling the Director at the earliest legal opportunity (after the final pass, if he is to be declarer or dummy, after play ends, if he is to be a defender), the player must inform the opponents that, in his opinion, his partner's explanation was erroneous.*

---

* Two examples may clarify responsibilities of the players (and the Director) after a misleading explanation has been given to the opponents. In both examples following, North has opened 1NT and South, who holds a weak hand with long diamonds, has bid 2♦, intending to sign off; North explains, however, in answer to West's inquiry, that South's bid is strong and artificial, asking for major suits.

### Example 1 — Mistaken Explanation

The actual partnership agreement is that 2♦ is a natural signoff; the mistake was in North's explanation. This explanation is an infraction of Law, since East-West are entitled to an accurate description of the North-South agreement (when this infraction results in damage to East-West, the Director shall award an adjusted score). If North subsequently becomes aware of his mistake, he must immediately notify the Director. South must do nothing to correct the mistaken explanation while the auction continues; after the final pass, South, if he is to be declarer or dummy, should call the Director and must volunteer a correction of the explanation. If South becomes a defender, he calls the Director and corrects the explanation when play ends.

### Example 2 — Mistaken Bid

The partnership agreement is as explained — 2♦ is strong and artificial; the mistake was in South's bid. Here there is no infraction of Law, since East-West did receive an accurate description of the North-South agreement; they have no claim to an accurate description of the North-South hands.

(Regardless of damage, the Director shall allow the result to stand; but the Director is to presume Mistaken Explanation, rather than Mistaken Bid, in the absence of evidence to the contrary.) South must not correct North's explanation (or notify the Director) immediately, and he has no responsibility to do so subsequently.

In both examples, South, having heard North's explanation, knows that his own 2♦ bid has been misinterpreted. This knowledge is "unauthorized information" (see Law 16A), so South must be careful not to base subsequent actions on this information (if he does, the Director shall award an adjusted score). For instance, if North rebids two notrump, South has the unauthorized information that this bid merely denies a four-card holding in either major suit; but South's responsibility is to act as though North had made a strong game try opposite a weak response, showing maximum values.

# LAW 76

## SPECTATORS

A. Conduct During Bidding or Play
　　1. One Hand Only
　　　　A spectator should not look at the hand of more than
　　　　one player, except by permission.
　　2. Personal Reaction
　　　　A spectator must not display any reaction to the bid-
　　　　ding or play while a deal is in progress.
　　3. Mannerisms or Remarks
　　　　During the round, a spectator must refrain from man-
　　　　nerisms or remarks of any kind (including conversa-
　　　　tion with a player).
　　4. Consideration for Players
　　　　A spectator must not in any way disturb a player.

B. Spectator Participation
　　A spectator may not call attention to any irregularity or
　　mistake, nor speak on any question of fact or law except
　　by request of the Director.

CHAPTER VIII

# **The Score**

## LAW 77
## DUPLICATE BRIDGE SCORING TABLE

### TRICK SCORE
Scored by declarer's side if the contract is fulfilled.

| IF TRUMPS ARE: | ♣ | ♦ | ♥ | ♠ |
|---|---|---|---|---|
| For each odd trick bid and made | | | | |
| Undoubled | 20 | 20 | 30 | 30 |
| Doubled | 40 | 40 | 60 | 60 |
| Redoubled | 80 | 80 | 120 | 120 |

| AT A NOTRUMP CONTRACT | UNDOUBLED | DOUBLED | REDOUBLED |
|---|---|---|---|
| For first odd trick bid and made | 40 | 80 | 160 |
| For each additional odd trick | 30 | 60 | 120 |

A trick score of 100 points or more, made on one board, is GAME. A trick score of less than 100 points is a PARTSCORE.

### PREMIUM SCORE
Scored by declarer's side
### SLAMS

| | Not Vulnerable | Vulnerable |
|---|---|---|
| For making a slam | | |
| Small Slam (12 tricks) bid and made | 500 | 750 |
| Grand Slam (all 13 tricks) bid and made | 1000 | 1500 |

### OVERTRICKS

| For each OVERTRICK | Not Vulnerable | Vulnerable |
|---|---|---|
| (tricks made in excess of contract) | | |
| Undoubled | Trick Value | Trick Value |
| Doubled | 100 | 200 |
| Redoubled | 200 | 400 |

### PREMIUMS FOR GAME, PARTSCORE, FULFILLING CONTRACT

| | |
|---|---|
| For making GAME vulnerable | 500 |
| For making GAME, not vulnerable | 300 |
| For making any PARTSCORE | 50 |
| For making any doubled, but not redoubled contract | 50 |
| For making any redoubled contract | 100 |

### UNDERTRICK PENALTIES
Scored by declarer's opponents if the contract is not fulfilled
### UNDERTRICKS
Tricks by which declarer falls short of the contract

| | Not Vulnerable | | | Vulnerable | | |
|---|---|---|---|---|---|---|
| | Undbld | Dbld | Rdbld | Undbld | Dbld | Rdbld |
| For first undertrick | 50 | 100 | 200 | 100 | 200 | 400 |
| For each additional undertrick | 50 | 200 | 400 | 100 | 300 | 600 |
| Bonus for the fourth and each subsequent undertrick | 0 | 100 | 200 | 0 | 0 | 0 |

# LAW 78

# METHODS OF SCORING

A. Matchpoint Scoring

In matchpoint scoring each contestant is awarded, for scores made by different contestants who have played the same board and whose scores are compared with his, two scoring units (matchpoints or half matchpoints) for each score inferior to his, one scoring unit for each score equal to his, and zero scoring units for each score superior to his.

B. International Matchpoint Scoring

In international matchpoint scoring, on each board the total point difference between the two scores compared is converted into IMPs according to the following scale.

| Difference in points | IMPs | Difference in points | IMPs | Difference in points | IMPs |
|---|---|---|---|---|---|
| 20–40 | 1 | 370–420 | 9 | 1500–1740 | 17 |
| 50–80 | 2 | 430–490 | 10 | 1750–1990 | 18 |
| 90–120 | 3 | 500–590 | 11 | 2000–2240 | 19 |
| 130–160 | 4 | 600–740 | 12 | 2250–2490 | 20 |
| 170–210 | 5 | 750–890 | 13 | 2500–2990 | 21 |
| 220–260 | 6 | 900–1090 | 14 | 3000–3490 | 22 |
| 270–310 | 7 | 1100–1290 | 15 | 3500–3990 | 23 |
| 320–360 | 8 | 1300–1490 | 16 | 4000 & upward | 24 |

C. Total Point Scoring

In total point scoring, the net total point score of all boards played is the score for each contestant.

D. Special Scoring Methods

Special scoring methods are permissible, if approved by the sponsoring organization. In advance of any contest the sponsoring organization should publish conditions of contest detailing conditions of entry, methods of scoring, determination of winners, breaking of ties, and the like.

## LAW 79

## TRICKS WON

A. Agreement on Tricks Won
The number of tricks won shall be agreed upon before all four hands have been returned to the board.

B. Disagreement on Tricks Won
If a subsequent disagreement arises, the Director must be called. No increase in score need be granted unless the Director is called before the round ends as specified in Law 8 (but Law 69 or Law 71 may supersede this provision when there has been an acquiescence or a concession).

C. Error in Score
An error in computing or tabulating the agreed-upon score, whether made by a player or scorer, may be corrected until the expiration of the period specified by the sponsoring organization. Unless the sponsoring organization specifies a later* time, this correction period expires 30 minutes after the official score has been made available for inspection.

---

* An earlier time may be specified when required by the special nature of a contest.

# CHAPTER IX

# Tournament Sponsorship

## LAW 80

### SPONSORING ORGANIZATION

A sponsoring organization conducting an event under these Laws has the following duties and powers:

A. Tournament Director
   to appoint the tournament Director. If there is no tournament Director, the players should designate one of their own number to perform his functions.

B. Advance Arrangements
   to make advance arrangements for the tournament, including playing quarters, accommodations and equipment.

C. Session Times
   to establish the date and time of each session.

D. Conditions of Entry
   to establish the conditions of entry.

E. Special Conditions
   to establish special conditions for bidding and play (such as written bidding, bidding boxes, screens — penalty provisions for actions not transmitted across a screen may be suspended).

F. Supplementary Regulations
   to publish or announce regulations supplementary to, but not in conflict with, these Laws.

G. Appeals
   To make suitable arrangements for appeals to be heard.

# CHAPTER X

# Tournament Director

## SECTION ONE
## RESPONSIBILITIES

## LAW 81

## DUTIES AND POWERS

A. Official Status

The Director is the official representative of the sponsoring organization.

B. Restrictions and Responsbilities
   1. Technical Management
      The Director is responsible for the technical management of the tournament.
   2. Observance of Laws and Regulations
      The Director is bound by these Laws and by supplementary regulations announced by the sponsoring organization.

C. Director's Duties and Powers
   The Director's duties and powers normally include the following:
   1. Assistants
      to appoint assistants, as required, to perform his duties.
   2. Entries
      to accept and list entries.
   3. Conditions of Play
      to establish suitable conditions of play and to announce them to the contestants.

4. Discipline
   to maintain discipline and to insure the orderly progress of the game.
5. Law
   to administer and interpret these Laws and to advise the players of their rights and responsibilities thereunder.
6. Errors
   to rectify an error or irregularity of which he becomes aware in any manner, within the correction period established in accordance with Law 79C.
7. Penalties
   to assess penalties when applicable.
8. Waiver of Penalties
   to waive penalties for cause, at his discretion, upon the request of the non-offending side.
9. Disputes
   to adjust disputes; to refer a matter to the appropriate committee.
10. Scores
    to collect scores and tabulate results.
11. Reports
    to report results to the sponsoring organization for official record.

D. Delegation of Duties
   The Director may delegate any of the duties listed in "C" to assistants, but he is not thereby relieved of responsibility for their correct performance.

## LAW 82

## RECTIFICATION OF ERRORS OF PROCEDURE

A. Director's Duty

It is the duty of the Director to rectify errors of procedure and to maintain the progress of the game in a manner that is not contrary to these Laws.

B. Rectification of Error

To rectify an error in procedure the Director may:
1. Award of Adjusted Score
   award an adjusted score as permitted by these Laws.
2. Specify Time of Play
   require or postpone the play of a board.

C. Director's Error

If the Director has given a ruling that he or the Chief Director subsequently determines to be incorrect, and if no rectification will allow the board to be scored normally, he shall award an adjusted score, considering both sides as non-offending for that purpose

## LAW 83

## NOTIFICATION OF THE RIGHT TO APPEAL

If the Director believes that a review of his decision on a point of fact or exercise of his discretionary power might be in order (as when he awards an adjusted score under Law 12), he shall advise a contestant of his right to appeal or may refer the matter to an appropriate committee.

# SECTION TWO
# RULINGS

## LAW 84

## RULINGS ON AGREED FACTS

When the Director is called to rule on a point of law or regulation in which the facts are agreed upon, he shall rule as follows:

A. No Penalty
   If no penalty is prescribed by law, and there is no occasion for him to exercise his discretionary powers, he directs the players to proceed with the auction or play.

B. Penalty under Law
   If a case is clearly covered by a Law that specifies a penalty for the irregularity, he assesses that penalty and sees that it is paid.

C. Player's Option
   If a Law gives a player a choice among penalties, the Director explains the options and sees that a penalty is selected and paid.

D. Director's Option
   If the Law gives the Director a choice between a specified penalty and the award of an adjusted score, he attempts to restore equity, resolving any doubtful point in favor of the non-offending side.

E. Discretionary Penalty
   If an irregularity has occurred for which no penalty is provided by law, the Director awards an adjusted score if

there is even a reasonable possibility that the non-offending side was damaged, notifying the offending side of its
right to appeal (see Law 81C9).

# LAW 85

## RULINGS ON DISPUTED FACTS

When the Director is called upon to rule on a point of
law or regulation in which the facts are not agreed upon, he
shall proceed as follows:

A. Director's Assessment
   If the Director is satisfied that he has ascertained the
   facts, he rules as in Law 84.

B. Facts Not Determined
   If the Director is unable to determine the facts to his satis-
   faction, he shall make a ruling that will permit play to
   continue, and notify the players of their right to appeal.

# SECTION THREE
# CORRECTION OF IRREGULARITIES

# LAW 86

## IN TEAM PLAY

A. Average Score at IMP Play
   When the Director chooses to award an artificial adjusted
   score of average plus or average minus in IMP play, that
   score is plus 3 IMPs or minus 3 IMPs respectively.

B. Non-balancing Adjustments, Knockout Play

When the Director assigns non-balancing adjusted scores (see Law 12C) in knockout play, each contestant's score on the board is calculated separately. The average of the two scores is then assigned to both contestants.

C. Substitute Board

The Director shall not exercise his Law 6 authority to order one board redealt when the final result of a match without that board could be known to a contestant. Instead, he awards an adjusted score.

# LAW 87

# FOULED BOARD

A. Definition

A board is considered to be "fouled" if the Director determines that one or more cards were misplaced in the board, in such manner that contestants who should have had a direct score comparison did not play the board in identical form.

B. Scoring the Fouled Board

In scoring a fouled board the Director determines as closely as possible which scores were made on the board in its correct form, and which in the changed form. He divides the score on that basis into two groups, and rates each group separately as provided in the regulations of the sponsoring organization.

In some forms of team contests, the sponsoring organization may prescribe a redeal (see Law 6).

# SECTION FOUR
# PENALTIES

## LAW 88

## AWARD OF INDEMNITY POINTS

In a pair or individual event, when a non-offending contestant is required to take an artificial adjusted score through no fault or choice of his own, such contestant shall be awarded a minimum of 60% of the matchpoints available to him on that board, or the percentage of matchpoints he earned on boards actually played during the session if that percentage was greater than 60%.

## LAW 89

## PENALTIES IN INDIVIDUAL EVENTS

In individual events, the Director shall enforce the penalty provisions of these Laws, and the provisions requiring the award of adjusted scores, equally against both members of the offending side, even though only one of them may be responsible for the irregularity. But the Director, in awarding adjusted scores, shall not assess procedural penalty points against the offender's partner, if, in the Director's opinion, he is in no way responsible for the violation.

# LAW 90

# PROCEDURAL PENALTIES

A. Director's Authority

The Director, in addition to enforcing the penalty provisions of these Laws, may also assess penalties for any offense that unduly delays or obstructs the game, inconveniences other contestants, violates correct procedure, or requires the award of an adjusted score at another table.

B. Offenses Subject to Penalty

Offenses subject to penalty include but are not limited to:

1. Tardiness

   arrival of a contestant after the specified starting time.

2. Slow Play

   unduly slow play by a contestant.

3. Loud Discussion

   discussion of the bidding, play or result of a board, which may be overheard at another table.

4. Comparing Scores

   unauthorized comparison of scores with another contestant.

5. Touching Another's Cards

   touching or handling of cards belonging to another player (Law 7).

6. Misplacing Cards in Board

   placing one or more cards in an incorrect pocket of the board.

7. Errors in Procedure

   errors in procedure (such as failure to count cards in one's hand, playing the wrong board, etc.) that require an adjusted score for any contestant.

8.  Failure to Comply
    failure to comply promptly with tournament regulations or with any instruction of the Director.

# LAW 91

## PENALIZE OR SUSPEND

A.  Director's Power
    In performing his duty to maintain order and discipline, the Director is specifically empowered to assess disciplinary penalties in points or to suspend a contestant for the current session or any part thereof (the Director's decision under this clause is final).

B.  Right to Disqualify
    The Director is specifically empowered to disqualify a contestant for cause, subject to approval by the Tournament Committee or sponsoring organization.

CHAPTER XI

# APPEALS

## LAW 92

### RIGHT TO APPEAL

A. Contestant's Right
   A contestant or his Captain may appeal for a review of any ruling made at his table by the Director*.

B. Time of Appeal
   The right to request or appeal a Director's ruling expires 30 minutes after the official score has been made available for inspection, unless the sponsoring organization has specified a different time period.

C. How to Appeal
   All appeals shall be made through the Director.

D. Concurrence of Appellants
   An appeal shall not be heard unless both members of a pair (except in an individual contest) or the captain of a team, concur in appealing. An absent member shall be deemed to concur.

---

* Sponsoring organizations may establish penalties for appeals without merit.

# LAW 93

# PROCEDURES OF APPEAL

A. No Appeals Committee
   The Chief Director shall hear and rule upon all appeals if there is no Tournament or Appeals Committee, or when a committee cannot meet without disturbing the orderly progress of the tournament.

B. Appeals Committee Available
   If a committee is available,
   1. Appeal Concerns Law
      The Chief Director shall hear and rule upon such part of the appeal as deals solely with the Law or regulations. His ruling may be appealed to the committee*.
   2. All Other Appeals
      The Chief Director shall refer all other appeals to the committee* for adjudication.
   3. Adjudication of Appeals
      In adjudicating appeals the committee* may exercise all powers assigned by these Laws to the Director, except that the committee may not overrule the Director on a point of law or regulations, or on exercise of his disciplinary powers. The committee may recommend to the Director that he change his ruling.

C. Appeal to National Authority
   After the preceding remedies have been exhausted, further appeal may be taken to the national authority (on a point of law, in ACBL the National Laws Commission, 2990 Airways Boulevard, Memphis, TN 38116-3847).

---

* Zonal organizations may establish differing conditions of appeals for special contests.

# Index to Duplicate Laws

## (REFERENCES ARE TO LAW NUMBERS)

# ELECTIONS BY THE ACBL BOARD OF DIRECTORS

Law 12 C.3: ACBL elects to specify otherwise. The provisions of this Law do not apply for ACBL (Zone 2) sanctioned contests.

Law 16 A.1: At ACBL sanctioned events, competitors will not be allowed to announce that they reserve the right to summon the Director later. They should summon the Director immediately when they believe there may have been extraneous information available to the opponents resulting in calls or bids which could result in damage to their side.

Law 18 F: The ACBL Board of Directors authorizes sponsoring organizations in Zone 2 to use bidding boxes. Any alternative method which is necessary to enable a person with a disability to compete is authorized subject to the approval of the Chief Director.

Law 40 D: One notrump openings with fewer than eight high-card points are barred in all ACBL sanctioned events.

Law 40 D: An opening one bid in a suit which by partnership agreement could show fewer than eight high-card points is not allowed. This does not apply to an opening bid intended as a psych.

Law 40 E. Both members of a partnership must employ the same system that appears on the convention card.
  1. During a session of play, a system may not be varied, except with permission of the tournament Director. (A Director might allow a pair to change a convention but would not allow a pair to change their basic system.)
  2. At the outset of a round or session, a pair may review their opponents' convention card and alter their defenses against the opponents' conventional calls and

preemptive bids. This must be announced to their opponents. The opponents may not vary their system after being informed of these alterations in defense.

Defenses to methods permitted by the ACBL Mid-Chart and/or SuperChart are designated as "unusual methods" and may be referred to during the auction.

Law 41 A & Law 45 A: Face-down opening leads are required at all ACBL sanctioned contests.

Law 61 B: The restriction that otherwise would prohibit defenders from asking one another whether they have a card of the suit led shall not apply, unless otherwise specified by action of the ACBL Board of Directors.

Law 93 B.1 The ACBL Board of Directors authorizes sponsoring organizations in Zone 2 to designate certain contests in which either of the following differing conditions of appeal may apply:

    1. The Chief Director shall hear and rule upon all appeals, or

    2. The Chief Director shall hear all appeals but may refer the matter to an appropriate committee.